Slightly Below the Glide Path
RAF Scampton

This book is dedicated to all who have served their King or Queen and country at RAF Scampton

First published in Great Britain in 2010
by Fox 3 Publishing York
YO32 3QX (69)
Updated July 2013

Printed in Great Britain by
Inky Little Fingers
Churcham
Gloucester
GL2 8AX

A catalogue record for this book is available from
The British Library

ISBN 978-0-9566319-0-9

Passing through Scampton Village heading towards Ingham you may notice on the left hand side, St John the Baptist's Church. Those with a keener eye may see the Cross of Sacrifice and the almost 100 white military headstones in the churchyard There is a general assumption that all the graves are of airmen who died in the Second World War and whilst this is true to some extent it is by no means the complete picture. The graves stand as a lasting memorial of how tragedy has visited Scampton over the past 70 years, with those buried bearing silent witness to the Royal Air Force's history in Lincolnshire from the Second World War, through the Cold War and on into the modern era.

"Slightly below the Glide Path - correcting nicely" are words that are familiar to all military pilots being talked down to land at an airfield in bad weather. This book takes its title from that procedure, as landing safely relied on being on the glide path. As this graveyard literally lies near the end of runway 05 at Scampton the title speaks for itself.

This book is about one of the most famous war time stations, RAF Scampton, the home of the 'Dambusters'. It's aim is to give you an insight into the station during the past 70 years or so through the eyes of those who sadly lost their lives and who will remain where they are forever, irrespective of what eventually happens to the station. It is right to keep their memory alive, pay them due respects and honour their service. They in turn have some fantastic stories to tell and now have that opportunity.

The Cross of Sacrifice was raised in Scampton Village Churchyard over the graves of sixty eight aircrew killed in the 1939-1945 War. Dedicated in July 1950 by the Lord Bishop of Lincoln it was unveiled by Air Marshal Sir Hugh Walmsley KCIE CB BE MC DFC in the presence of the Air Officer Commanding and the Station Commander. The Air Marshal had commanded Scampton in 1940. The above picture was taken not long after the unveiling.

Introduction

Scampton's military connections stretch back nearly 2000 years. To the Romans, the A15 which runs alongside the station was known as Ermine Street and was a major military highway connecting the Roman city of Lindum (Lincoln) to the rest of the empire. In 1795, a Roman villa was discovered not far from the site of what was to become RAF Scampton. RAF Scampton's crest still reflects this connection to its Roman heritage; the design is of a bow and arrow on a blue background. The string of the bow represents Ermine Street and the curved bow represents the diversion that the A15 had to take when the airfield was expanded in the 1950's. The arrow is orientated to show Scampton's main runway and the blue disc depicts the sky. The Latin motto of "Armatus Non Lacessitur" is one that a Roman soldier could easily have identified with, "an armed man is not attacked".

The link with aviation began in 1916 when a searchlight battery was based on the site. Later in the same year, the first aircraft flew from the station, which at that time was known as Brattleby. Throughout World War One Scampton's main function was the training of new pilots for the western front. However, when the war ended, so did Scampton's usefulness and by 1919 all the station buildings had been demolished. Today, no trace remains of Scampton's First World War history.

By the 1930's, war was once again on the horizon and the Air Ministry began its preparations. In what was to become known as the expansion period, it was announced that a bomber airfield would be constructed at Scampton. From the announcement in 1935 it was barely a year before the first flying unit arrived. The aircraft were Handley Page Heyfords (opposite) and given that the country was only 3 years away from war with a technologically advanced enemy, they were hopelessly outdated.

4

In the nick of time, barely a year before the outbreak of war, Scampton's two resident squadrons, 49 and 83 received a light bomber of modern design. The Handley Page Hampden, although considered modern by the RAF, was still hopelessly obsolete compared to the cutting edge fighters which the German Luftwaffe were fielding. Consequently losses were heavy, but the crews soldiered on with the Hampden until 1942. It was during the Hampden era that the station gained two of its three Victoria Crosses. The recipients were Flight Lieutenant Learoyd of 49 Squadron and Sergeant Hannah of 83 Squadron.

Scampton's airmen must have been mightily relieved when their new aircraft, the much vaunted Avro Manchester, (right) became operational in January 1942. However, this was to prove a false dawn as the Manchester was a dreadful aircraft, prone to engine failures. Out of the failure of the Manchester was born the Lancaster, and by July 1942 both Squadrons finally had an award winning aircraft. (Below)

On 16th May 1943, the 19 Lancasters of 617 Squadron secured the station's place in history. The breaching of the Ruhr dams was not only a triumph of flying skill and technology, but also a much needed boost to the morale of the country. Once again, the cost was heavy and 8 Lancaster crews never returned to Scampton. Their leader, Wing Commander Guy Gibson was awarded the Victoria Cross for this mission, bringing the station's tally to three; a feat no other RAF station has ever achieved.

His Majesty King George VI with Wing Commander G. P. Gibson VC DSO DFC to his right and Scampton Station Commander Group Captain JNH Whitworth DSO DFC to his left on a visit to Scampton just after the Dam Buster raids. One of the modified Lancaster bombers is to the rear of them.

The Dambuster's had departed from the station's grass runway, but to realise the Lancaster's true potential concrete runways were needed. The airfield closed for a period whilst the runways were built, but the Lancasters were soon to return and it was with this aircraft that Scampton finished the war.

Post war, the station played host to B29 Superfortresses of the United States Air Force and subsequently the Avro Lincoln. In 1953, RAF Scampton entered the jet-age with the arrival of the English Electric Canberra. In 1955, Scampton embarked on its most ambitious expansion since the 1930's. The catalyst for this work was the imminent

Above: Officers outside the Officers' Mess at Scampton in the Spring of 1960.
Below: The nuclear Vulcan force at Scampton

Two photographs of the Blue Steel Missile Servicing Bays at Scampton

arrival of the Avro Vulcan and the nuclear weapons it would carry. The work involved the extension of the runway and an extensive building programme across the station. The work was completed in 1958 and the first Vulcan arrived shortly afterwards.

After the station's Vulcan's were retired from service in 1982, the next major residents were the Central Flying School. Along with them came the RAF Aerobatic Team, known to all as the Red Arrows. The Red Arrows are still in residence at the time of writing, but not for the first time it is uncertain how long they will remain.

The Royal Air Force Aerobatic Team -The Red Arrows

What the future holds for RAF Scampton is unclear, it certainly seems that its use as an RAF station is coming to an end. Whatever happens in the future, it has earned a permanent place in the history of the RAF and will continue to epitomise all that it stands for, long after the last serviceman has left. However, the servicemen we write about in this book who gave their lives in the service of their country, will remain forever and always be a reminder of the presence of the Royal Air Force at Scampton. On behalf of a grateful nation - May they Rest in Peace.

The Royal Air Force Standard which flies proudly inside St John the Baptist's Church at Scampton

High Flight

Oh! I have slipped the surly bonds of Earth
And danced the skies on laughter-silvered wings;
Sunward I've climbed, and joined the tumbling
mirth
Of sun-split clouds, — and done a hundred things
You have not dreamed of — wheeled and soared
and swung
High in the sunlit silence. Hov'ring there,
I've chased the shouting wind along, and flung
My eager craft through footless halls of air. . . .

Up, up the long, delirious burning blue
I've topped the wind-swept heights with easy grace
Where never lark, or ever eagle flew —
And, while with silent, lifting mind I've trod
The high untrespassed sanctity of space,
Put out my hand, and touched the face of God.

John Gillespie Magee Jr.

John Gillespie Magee Jr. was an RAF pilot, born of an American father and English mother. He was flying a Spitfire on a high altitude test flight and whilst descending from 30,000 feet was inspired to put together his now famous prose. Magee flew from RAF Digby, not very many miles from Scampton and had shared the privilege of flying in the skies over Lincolnshire with many of the airmen in this book. Like many of them Magee also died tragically in those same skies when on 11th December 1941 his Spitfire AD 291 was descending through cloud and collided with an Oxford aircraft from RAF Cranwell. He was too low to bale out successfully. He was just 19 years of age.

Identifying Military Grave Markers

The vast majority of burials at Scampton fall under the responsibility of the Commonwealth War Graves Commission. The Commission was founded by Royal Charter in 1917 and now tends to the graves of 1.7 million service men and women that were killed in both World Wars. The headstones that fall under the responsibility of the Commission are generally made of Portland Stone (Although they do vary around the world) and can be identified by the way the top of the headstone is rounded with a single continuous dome. The rank and name of the deceased, date of death and the service / Regiment they were in together with the crest of the service / Regiment appear on each stone. Many of the smaller sites in England, such as Scampton are subcontracted to local churches etc. to maintain.

There are also a number of German graves at Scampton, and these are maintained to the same standard as those of our own airmen. The stones are much simpler and state only the name of the deceased, their date of birth and the date they died. The stone features a German cross at the top. The one shown has two names on. The full explanation is in the book.

Post war, the grave stones changed and these can be identified by what is a humped dome at the top of the headstone. These graves fall under the responsibility of the Department of the Environment.

Hopefully, if you can, you will wander around the churchyard, pause and reflect on the souls who lay beneath your feet and allow this book to tell you their story, not only about themselves but their families and loved ones where we have been able to be privy to this information. What follows are our efforts to allow you to peep into their lives, often short lived and see the person below the stone. If you cannot visit then please allow this book to guide you there in spirit.

Corporal Thomas Alexander Keating
Wireless Operator
Leading Aircraftman Walter Gerald Kelly
Wireless Operator
Aircraftman First Class Stanley Taylor
Wireless Operator

23rd November 1939

World War Two was barely 3 months old when the Royal Air Force first had occasion to use Scampton Saint John the Baptist Church as a burial place. T h e 23rd November was a typical November day, cold and foggy, with visibility down to just 50 yards. The weather was so bad that at first the 49 Squadron Commanding Officer had considered cancelling what was to become the fatal flight, but upon hearing that the pilot was Squadron Leader McGregor-Watt, he was reassured and allowed it to go ahead. The squadron commander had good reason to be confident in his pilot. Squadron Leader McGregor-Watt was very experienced having been trained at the prestigious Royal Air Force College at Cranwell. He had been a pilot for just under thirteen years and had in that time amassed over 3000 hours flying.

For Squadron Leader McGregor-Watt today's duty was to take Hampden L4034 from Scampton to Waddington where his three trainee wireless operators could practice ZZ landings under the guidance of their instructor Corporal Keating. Due to the local nature of the flight, it was not considered necessary to have a second pilot or navigator onboard. ZZ was a blind approach system designed to allow an aircraft to land in bad weather, the initials standing for Zero visibility and Zero Cloud-base. In the days before radar it was a rudimentary, but essential means of landing the aircraft in poor visibility. The wireless operator would receive several radio bearings transmitted from the control tower on the airfield. These bearings would allow the pilot to work out his position relative to the airfield and line-up for a landing.

At around noon disaster struck. Having apparently misjudged the approach the twin engine Hampden roared across the airfield with its engines at full power and flying at only ten feet above the ground. In a desperate bid to avoid the control tower, which had appeared in front of him, the pilot put the aircraft into a steep bank to the right. Despite narrowly missing the control tower the pilot was unable to avoid one of the airfield hangars and crashed onto its roof. The aircraft skipped across the roof before plunging to the ground. All those on board the aircraft were killed on impact or died shortly afterwards.

Sadly this accident also caused casualties on the ground. Three airmen of Waddington's 50 Squadron, who had been working in number two hangar were killed when one of the engines from the aircraft fell through the roof onto their work area.

LAC Walter Gerald Kelly

Investigations into the accident established that the radio, which transmitted the bearings to the pilot, was poorly sighted and this directly led to the crash. As a consequence the transmitter was re-sited and procedures improved to prevent future accidents.

The aircraft involved had been the first Hampden to be delivered to Bomber Command on 20th September 1938, making it just over one year old at the time of the crash. While Corporal Keating who was from Winchester was relatively old at 46, those killed in the hangar were much younger. Corporal Archibald MacDonald Henderson was 24 and a native of Gosforth, Newcastle upon Tyne. He is buried with other RAF colleagues just outside RAF Waddington in St Michael's Churchyard (Shown below). Aircraftman First Class Leslie McGarvie is buried in Prestwich whilst Aircraftman Second Class Frank Talbot, who was only 18 years old, is buried in Blackburn Cemetery.

Ernest Kelly (Left) with his father

Aircraftman Second Class M. Bastow was injured; however, the extent of his injuries are not known, but he appears to have survived the war. Although most of the crew of L4034 were buried at Scampton, the pilot, Squadron Leader McGregor-Watt was buried close to Scampton in All Saints New Church, Nettleham. Although it can't be said with certainty this is more than likely because he lived in the village. Walter Kelly's grave is still visited by his family and through the memoirs of his brother Ernest, a fascinating insight into the background from which Walter came can be gained.

Extract from Ernest Kelly's Memoirs

Our parents through all this were hard working people who worked from 6am to 6pm daily with Saturday morning 6am to noon and one weeks paid holiday per year (if you had worked for 51 weeks prior). The pay was poor and the families arge, but we ate well and enjoyed ourselves even without televisions, motor cars and the like. Holidays consisted of a day at Wetherby Races, a visit to the park or left to our own devices, a trip to Shipley Glen.

At school we learnt to speak English (with a Yorkshire accent), some French,which consisted of a few standard phrases and enough maths to enable us to count our pocket money (6 pence a week if you ran errands for the neighbours).

Father was a Mill Wright, locally known as a Mill Mechanic. We always respected him for a hard working man who knew his job thoroughly and could turn his hand to almost any do it yourself chores. Our shoes were made by him from cut-off drive belt leather used on textile machinery. He lacked academic knowledge but made up for it in basic wisdom and know-how.

Pilot Officer Oliver Harry Launders
Pilot

8th July 1940

Pilot Officer Launders took-off from Scampton at 9:50pm on 7th July 1940 as the pilot of 83 Squadron Hampden L4066. His target carried the code A 161 but to him and his crew, that meant bombing Frankfurt in Germany.

That night he was part of a force of fifty-four aircraft attacking Germany and Holland, but his aircraft was to be the only one lost. Early the next day it crashed three miles north east of Clacton. One of the crew of four, Sergeant Leonard Howard initially survived the crash but died soon afterwards. He is buried in Liverpool (Ford) Roman Catholic Cemetery. The pilot and the two Observers, Sergeant Cyril Hallett and Sergeant Basil Kinton were killed instantly. Kinton was just 18 years old. They are buried at All Saints Churchyard, Woodford and Priory Road Cemetery, Huntington respectively.

Aircraftman Second Class Robert William Bennett

20th July 1940

The Battle of Britain was at its height, but it was not just the Luftwaffe who were claiming their victims, others died of more indirect causes. Blackout restrictions at the time not only required that street lighting be extinguished, but also that the owners of cars mask-off their headlights, so that just a narrow beam of light was produced.

It was late on the evening of Saturday 20th July 1940 when Robert Bennett aged twenty four and originally from Wilfred Avenue, Rainham in Essex, was walking along the Lincoln to Market Rasen Road. He had just caught up with Private Edwin Atkinson and they were chatting as they returned home to Dunholme Lodge, from Nettleham. Both men were walking on the left-hand side of the road with their backs to the traffic, Robert to the right of Edwin. It was a dark night and clouds obscured the moon.

Major Urwin of the Royal Engineers and his driver, co-incidentally, also named Bennett, were travelling in the same direction at a speed of about 30 miles an hour. As they rounded an S-bend in their car, they suddenly saw two figures appear out of the darkness; their much-reduced headlights would have made this a very late sighting indeed. Major Urwin later estimated it to be only a few feet. It seemed certain that the car would hit both men but the driver swerved to the right and managed to avoid Private Atkinson. Robert Bennett was less fortunate and after being struck by the car was then rushed to Lincoln County Hospital. He suffered a fractured thighbone and a fractured skull. Sadly, he died 20 minutes after admission to the hospital.

At the time of the accident, Atkinson only heard a bump and was shocked to see Robert lying, badly injured, in the verge. In his evidence to the coroner Atkinson stated that he hadn't heard the car coming and that he had never been sure which side of the road pedestrians were supposed to walk on at night. Major Unwin told the court that his driver, Bennett had been on active service with him in France and that he considered him a careful and reliable man.

The coroner reminded the public of the dangers of walking with their backs to the traffic, especially at night. The inquest also revealed that the accident had nearly been avoided completely. Police Sergeant Lewis stated "The accident occurred about half way around an S bend. From the position of the marks, it appeared that the driver had nearly avoided the accident completely". A verdict of accidental death was returned and the jury exonerated the driver.

Sergeant Harry Alexander Bowmer

2nd August 1940

Lincolnshire was the spiritual home of Bomber Command and Lincoln itself was definitely the place where bomber crews liked to go to enjoy an evening's relaxation. When operations were off for the night the pubs of Lincoln were always full of RAF aircrew. Most belonged to Bomber Command, but there were also a small number of fighter pilots. A favourite haunt for both was the Saracen's Head Hotel, known at the time as the Snake Pit.

In his book Enemy Coast Ahead, Guy Gibson vividly describes the nightlife in the city and even reveals a tale of rivalry between the bomber crews and their counterparts in Fighter Command. In what he calls the Battle of the Snake Pit, what started as friendly banter and rivalry soon escalated into a full-scale war.

Over a period of some months, bomber and fighter crews staged a series of tit-for-tat raids respectively. These raids steadily escalated from hats being stolen from the Officers' Mess to the bombing of RAF Digby with toilet rolls. Proceedings were finally called to a halt after the kidnap of Scampton's Station Commander, who was taken by the fighter pilots to Digby and made to pick up the toilet rolls with a stick. It was then decided that Fighter and Bomber Command were in danger of doing more damage to each other than the enemy.

On 2nd August 1940 it seems that Sergeant Harry Bowmer, a Hampden crewman from 83 Squadron, had planned a much quieter evening. He and two colleagues had gone to the City Hotel on the Cornhill in Lincoln for a couple of drinks. When the bar closed at 10pm Harry and his friends invited Bertha Spencer, a barmaid at the Hotel and her friend Miss Jacklin to go with them to a local milk bar.

Airmen enjoying a few beers

At 11pm, the group returned to the City Hotel where Bertha lived. After chatting for a few minutes, they said goodnight and the group parted, going their separate ways. Rather strangely, Harry returned some minutes later and rang the doorbell to the hotel. Arthur Scott, the hotel proprietor interrupted his supper to answer the door.

He recalled at the later inquest that Harry did not say what he wanted and left a few minutes later. Scott knew Harry as a regular customer and had served him several drinks earlier that night. However, he went on to state quite categorically that he certainly wasn't drunk.

By 11:30pm Mr Scott had gone to bed. Not long afterwards he heard a crash and went downstairs to investigate. On opening the door he found Harry unconscious on the street with severe injuries. He had fractured his skull, broken his forearm and dislocated his hip. Harry who was 21 died two days later in the County Hospital in Lincoln.

The Coroner established that Harry appeared to have climbed a drainpipe and had slipped from a 2-inch ledge beneath a kitchen window, on the second floor. In court Miss Spencer maintained that she had not made an appointment with Harry and could not think why he had climbed the drainpipe. The Coroner was equally perplexed and despite saying that Harry was a quiet and sensible young man, he concluded that he had no one but himself to blame for what he called a silly prank.

Perhaps this was a little harsh, it may be that for someone who was facing imminent death on a nightly basis, the climb up a drainpipe didn't seem all that dangerous.

Pilot Officer Clifford Molyneux Lochhead
Navigator

19th September 1940

Clifford Lochhead was a twenty-year-old navigator on 49 Squadron. He died after a motorcycle accident at Scampton on 19th September 1940. This was particularly unfortunate, as he had survived a close brush with death only three months earlier when on the 8th June 1940 his Hampden suffered severe engine problems just after take-off. The aircraft was to crash at Carlton Hill just to the north west of Lincoln.

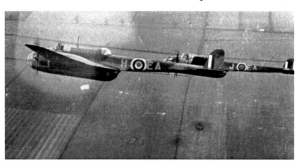

All four crew were injured in the process. He was to recover from his injuries and return to flying duties where he may have expected to die, not as he sadly did, in an accident on the roads of Lincolnshire.

49 Squadron Hampdens on low level exercises 1940

Pilot Officer Dudley Delacourtte Snooke
Pilot

28th September 1940

Pilot Officer Snooke's mission was to take his 83 Squadron Hampden to Lorient in France and attack the U-Boat pens there. Although it was still early in the war, the twenty year-old South African would have known only too well that Hitler's U-Boats were going to be a major threat. An island nation could not last long if the sea-lanes around it were infested with the Reich's silent killers.

In total, twelve aircraft were dispatched to Lorient of which nine located and attacked their target. It would seem that Pilot Officer Snooke was one of those who had not found the target and returned with his bombs still on board. Arriving back over Lincolnshire in the early hours of Saturday 28th September 1940 he and his crew were unable to locate the airfield at Scampton. Running desperately short of fuel, at 3:50am he ordered the aircraft to be abandoned.

His crew parachuted to safety but 20 year old Pilot Officer Snooke was not so lucky. Reports vary, but his parachute either became entangled with the doomed aircraft or he became impaled on railings on landing. In any case, his body was found a short distance from the crash site at Saint Mathias Church on the corner of Burton Road and Yarborough Crescent in Lincoln.

Contemporary reports indicate that the aircraft's impact caused a large explosion, which woke most of Lincoln. The church was extensively damaged, evidence of which can still be seen today which bears this out. The survivors from the aircraft were Pilot Officer Eric Clarke, Pilot Officer Charles Laurence Turner and Sergeant Kenneth McKenzie.

In recent years the pupils of Broadgate Junior School in Lincoln, close to the site of the crash, researched this Incident. In tribute to Pilot Officer Snooke the pupils designed a memorial in the form of a broken Hampden, which is now on display at the entrance to the school.

Hampden ground crew at Scampton

Private Tom Horberry

28th September 1940

On the same day as Pilot Officer Snooke lost his life, Tom Horberry was walking from Dunholme to Welton with two friends. But whilst he was walking in the dark, a bus of the Lincolnshire Road Car Company driven by Albert Shadlock struck him.   Tom was the second victim of a road accident in two months, both of which had been due, at least in part, to the blackout. Mr Shadlock was exonerated of blame by the Coroner at the subsequent inquest.

As a Private in the King's Own Yorkshire Light Infantry, Tom Horberry is the only member of the army to be buried at Scampton. At the time, the Regiment fielded several light anti-aircraft batteries at Scampton and it would seem most likely that this was his posting.

What was it like to be on Ops?

During the Second World War Eric Clarke was a Wireless Operator / Air Gunner (WOp /AG) and flew missions out of Scampton in Hampden and later Manchester and Lancaster bombers of 49 Squadron. In 2009 aged 96 he returned to the skies courtesy of the RAF Waddington Flying Club and landed once again at RAF Scampton, his last landing there being October 24th 1943, at which time the runways were grass. His pilot on the day was co-author of this book, Flight Lieutenant Gary Mennell. Eric kindly wrote the following account of his memories of what it was like to be on operations:

What was it like to be on Ops? How often has this question been asked? On Sunday the 21st September 1941 I arrived at RAF Scampton, along with another WOp / AG Sgt Patrick Maloney (an Irish Cockney) having completed a 12 week course of operational training at No.16 OTU at RAF Upper Heyford

Eric Clarke (Left) with Gary Mennell

on Handley Page Hampdens. I was to learn later that our course, No 21 I think, suffered the most losses in training.

Pat and I became very good friends and left Scampton on the same day Friday the 13th 1942 having completed 14 months on operations. He was posted north to RAF Lossiemouth and I was posted south to RAF Pershore, 23 OTU. I did not see him again until August 1943 when he called to see me at my unit on his way home on leave - I was a Flight Lieutenant, he was a Flying Officer. We were both very lucky survivors. But Pat did not survive. He volunteered for a second tour (with 83 Sqn I think). In August 1944 I received a letter from his brother informing me that Pat and crew baled out over Lincolnshire, but Pat`s parachute failed to open. His crew survived only to go missing on a further Op. Some years ago I found that Pat was buried in a North London Cemetery with his Mother and I visited the grave. The War Grave Commission headstone was almost covered in weeds. I learned that the Cemetery had been sold for £1. Pat had gained Flight Lieutenant rank and had been awarded the Distinguished Flying Medal.

On arrival at Scampton we carried out the arrival procedure which consisted of visiting certain Sections and signing in. The final visit was to Station Headquarters which, among other things, ensured we were on the payroll. We were billeted in the former married quarters. The following morning we found our way to the Wireless Operators crew room in No.2 Hangar, which looked out on the airfield. There were

about twenty WOp/AGs consisting of A and B Flights where Flight Sergeant Jack Gadsby said we were in his Flight - A. Flight Sgt Wally Ellis who had a DFM and Bar was NCO in charge of A Flight. I learned later that both Ellis and Gadsby joined the Squadron in 1938, and that Jack Gadsby had done his first Op as an LAC, before all aircrew were made Sergeants. He also had a DFM and was on his second tour. Jack and about five or six others would be in their late 20`s the rest seemed to be quite young, around age 20. Pat and I were both 28   - old boys!.- new boys!

The Hampden bomber had a crew of 4 - Pilot, Navigator (who also combined Bomb Aimer) Wireless Operator and Rear Gunner. Apparently there were no `straight` Air Gunners, so the crew comprised Pilot, Navigator and 2 Wireless Ops. One WOp would be `on the set` in the upper position and the other in the lower gun position, known as `the Tin`.

Eric in flying kit during the war

What was it like being on Ops? I was not to know until Monday 13th October 1941. Normally, we got word in the crew room by 9am that aircraft, say nine, were serviceable and F/S Jack Gadsby would detail us to carry out a DI (daily inspection) on a specific aircraft and usually it would be the aircraft that you later flew in to certify its fitness for an operation. This involved a ten to fifteen minute flight with the pilot, usually the same pilot with whom you would fly that night, but this did not always happen.

Later in the morning, we could see from our crew room window a tractor towing a string of bomb trolleys and we might just get an inkling of the type of operation that night. Ruhr, happy valley!! or mining known as gardening, but we just speculated. Sometimes F/S Jack Gadsby would be able to say that you were flying with such a Pilot in , say , K King. The rest of us would not know until we saw the Ops board at briefing but if your Pilot was an NCO, he would know and he would contact you, but if your Pilot was an Officer you would not see him until briefing.

There were a few occasions in the early days, where a crew stayed together in the Hampdens, but not many. The merits of the Pilots were certainly discussed in the WOps crew room , comments like "spot on" "Super" "Wizard" and so on but also not so others who might merit "Dopey" "Crazy and other unspeakable sorts. Obviously, affinities were formed but of a tenuous nature.

When we got the Manchesters, we had seven crew and the majority stayed together, but we might not see much of the Officer members until we assembled for boarding. They had their own crew rooms

When Pat and I walked into the WOps crew room that first morning I must say I felt a sense of disappointment. The room was full of blue smoke with a crowd of WOps looking somewhat dishevelled sitting round small tables playing cards or dominoes, and the floor looked as if it had not been swept for weeks. Battle dress had not yet been issued and they looked a very untidy lot.

Somehow I expected something different, however Pat and I fitted in and got to know the routine. I stuck it for a week or two and then arranged with Pat to go down with me early one morning and clean the place up. We tipped all the tables and chairs out on the grass frontage, borrowed some sweeping brushes from the hangar staff and gave the

Bombing up a Hampden

place a thorough clean up, much to the surprise of the arriving WOps. I suggested to F/S Jack Gadsby that a cleaning rota be set up and he agreed. I asked his permission to re-arrange the notice board and he agreed. The first time I got home on a `48` I returned armed with card, lettering pens etc and set the board up afresh.

The daytime was a mixture of DI`s NFT`s, a lecture, parachute re-packing, and some local flying, otherwise it was cards and dominoes for some. I only occasionally joined in when pressed, but always refused to gamble. Pat was of the same mind. Amazingly, I did not get airborne until the 12th October, actually 0010 hrs on the 13th on an op!

I had not been informed that I was flying that night until F/S Gadsby told me at teatime to be at briefing 1800 hrs.

Arriving at briefing I found I was crewed with a Sergeant Pilot Robinson, Navigator Sgt Black, and Wireless Operator Sgt Mossop. I was in the Tin. The target was Halse (also called Huls) and it was to be my first flight with 49 Squadron and it was to be an Operation.

I did not know the Pilot or Navigator, but of course I knew the WOp Sgt Mossop. He was a buddy of F/S Gadsby and a `Veteran`.

Aircrew de-briefing after a mission

I did not know it at the time, but in September, Sgt Robinson and crew including Sgt Mossop, crashed short of petrol near Banff in Scotland and all the crew were injured. They were part of a force flying from Lossiemouth to lay mines in the approaches to Oslo Fford where the German battleship Von Scheer was moored.

Later, in December Sgt Robinson and crew crash landed at Bircham Newton in Norfolk after a raid on Bremerhavenn in which Sgt Black was killed by a cannon shell. (The others were unhurt.)

The briefing was short, the Squadron Commander pointing out the target and the reason for the operation, the route out and back, followed by specialist Officers, meteorologist, navigator signals and intelligence.

Take-off times were also announced, then the individual crews got into a huddle over the navigator's chart after which we returned to our Messes for a `night flying supper`.

There was no excitement, just quiet conversation and discussion.

We all met at 2300 hours in front of the Hangar, fully kitted up, extra jerseys and the like as it was very cold in the Hampden and along came the Wagon. No more smoking, cigarettes stubbed out.

An officer would sit in front with the WAAF driver and we piled in, 2 or 3 crews at a time and we were off to dispersal. No sign of `nerves' but quite a lot of banter. I think. to some of the younger ones, it was an adventure of a sort with little thought of the possible horrors. You would hear "I have done 10 now, how many have you done?" or "Get some in" or similar. I did not announce it was my first.

The pilot, who, at this time was addressed as `Skipper` was in conversation with the ground crew Flight Sergeant, after which he just said "Lets get going". All this was in `black out` conditions and then the sound of engines starting up and some shouting.

The pilot and navigator entered through the front hatch the Wireless Operator and myself through the rear lower gun position - the Tin. I was the last. We were all in and individually commenced connecting up routines. I stowed my chute, checked the safety catches on my guns - twin Vickers gas operated, plugged in the oxygen tube, a bayonet type, and then listened in to the crew checking intercom contact with each other but firstly with the Pilot. "Hello Skipper, navigator here" and similar from the WOp and myself. Good intercom was so vital, just one defective headset could cause the whole intercom to fail and possibly the whole operation. For take-off and landing the Tin ` gunner had to squeeze in with the Wireless Op.

The engines were started up, with some vibration as they were warmed up and we checked the intercom again, and then we commenced the taxiing to take off.

Waiting for take off, I found myself musing, if that is the right word. I went back to the time , while at Yatesbury Wireless School, I hitch hiked home on a `48` and found myself on the London North Circular Road, making my way to a Lorry Park at Finchley where I could get a lift up the A1 to Yorkshire through the night.

The All Clear had just sounded and I had to wend my way (incidentally with a veteran hitch hiker who certainly knew his way around, through bomb damage), with fire engines and others doing their job, burst water mains, shop windows out, glass and goods all over the place. Maybe because we were in uniform the Wardens took no notice of us.

As I sat in my bomber I began to ask myself what damage were we going to do I also remembered when on leave, the red sky over Sheffield some 18 miles away. I thought of the reports by radio and news papers of the damage and countless civilian deaths in London and our big cities.

Why was I here, listening to the engines of my bomber about to take off to do untold damage and death to another people. I consoled myself that my country was fighting for its very existence, and that I was a very small cog in a massive war machine. Germany had over run Europe and England could be the next victim. So horrible to think and yet possible?

With these and other thoughts I began to ask myself "What happens now?" Are we going to be successful and carry out our mission with a safe return, to do more? Or are we going to be shot down - shall I have to bale out?

I had no qualms about baling out, but would I be able to? I certainly feared coming down in the sea? We now know that the North Sea is a graveyard of hundreds of our bombers.

My musings are interrupted, "OK boys we are off" and with a surge of the engines we rumble down the runway, gathering speed and then the rumbling ceases and we sense a slight lift - we are airborne and I feel as if I am sweating. Some people say "God defend the right "but as I muse I hear the Navigator telling the Pilot "Wheels up OK". and then reminds him of the compass course to the coast.

Bill Mossop gave me a `thumbs up` signal and I clambered down to my lower gun position, and then re-checked my intercom. During the steady climb I swung my guns from side to side checking my view and began musing again. I did not want this, I wanted to be on the set, however, my turn will come.

We were now flying level and the engines droned, what is to be will be??!!. My thoughts flew home, to my wife. Past midnight she would be in bed. We married in 1937. I was 24 she 21 and we lived with her widowed mother and right now we are expecting our first child - about the end of December, I suddenly felt very much alone, isolated, apprehensive?

What am I doing here? When War broke out I knew I was of military age and in the 1930`s, as I worked in a Doncaster office I got used to seeing various aircraft flying around and in 1936 RAF Finningley (5 miles south of Doncaster) opened and I also got used to seeing `the boys in blue` in the town, mostly wearing an aircrew brevet, Pilot, Observer etc. and the aircraft were Handley Page Hampdens.

I did not fancy myself with a Lee Enfield .303 plus bayonet and I had some ideas about becoming one of those `boys` so at the first opportunity I visited the recruiting office at Sheffield and applied for aircrew navigation but was refused on the spot as I did not have Grammar School education, but I was offered `Wireless Operator / Air Gunner which I accepted. I was called up on 13th August 1940. My wife and I had decided not to have children - because of the War - but when I commenced flying training she changed her mind and now we awaited our first child.

Suddenly I heard the Navigator give the Pilot a new course, we were crossing the Norfolk coast, good bye England! Hopefully just for the time being.

I think we were at about 10 to 12 thousand feet, and the Navigator sounded crisp and confident and the W/Op reported `nothing from Group. Throughout the trip the W/Op must listen out to Group H.Q. every 15 minutes from the hour in case of recall or diversion, W/T silence was observed except in case of emergency and only then with the Pilot's permission. As we approached the enemy coast the Pilot warned us that we were in a night fighter zone, but there was now a lot of cloud and I could see nothing. My first operation. In the next 14 months I was to survive twenty six operations with nine different pilots, in three different bombers, Hampdens, Manchesters and Lancasters.

The Air Ministry report reads: " AD979 Sgt. Robinson,10/10th cloud at Wesel on ETA, set course for Target, dropped flare without success for 25 minutes at 2000 -4000 ft looking for target spending fifty minutes in area, Essen and Ruhr under 10/10th cloud, bombed drome and flare path in Holland on return."

We landed at base at 0750 hrs, we had been airborne 6 hrs 20 mins. We piled into the waiting wagon, went to de-briefing and then to breakfast, somebody said everybody back. With a strange sense of elation I went to bed. In the billet Pat was just leaving for breakfast - he had not been on that Op.

The next day I was able to have a talk with Bill Mossop, the W/op, and discussed the flight. He laconically summed it up as " a fat lot of good!!" He said he was about finished and I don`t remember seeing him again. I think he had completed his tour. There was constant `movement` in the W/Ops crew room - on leave, on a course, failing to return, new arrivals. One Sergeant arrived (Sgt Way) who made it known that he was expecting his commission to come through. He was on the Channel Dash detail the same week and did not return. He was posted missing as Pilot Officer W S Way. We lost fifteen NCO aircrew, including seven W/Ops.

My second Op was with Sgt. Pilot Bow and a different crew - I didn't know if they were veterans or new boys. The target was Mannheim and the Air Ministry report reads " Flak and searchlight opposition over Belgian coast, cloud necessitated flying at 18000 ft. Target bombed at 14000 ft and pin point at river junction seen. Electrical storms prevailed over target area". We diverted on the return to Horsham St. Faith in Norfolk in pouring rain. We slept in the Sergeants Mess lounge and flew back to Scampton next morning. On the Op we took off at 1800 hrs and were airborne 7 hrs 35 mins. I was able to receive Group HQ transmissions but I would not have been able to transmit if required due to heavy static. I went on to do nine more Ops (raids) one in the Tin and eight on the Wireless, with six different Pilots, including two with Squadron Leader P D S Bennett DFC our B Flight Commander. I was happy to be on the set and felt that I was really doing the job I was trained to do.

Sergeant Frederick Norman Colin Catley
Pilot
Sergeant Bertram Victor Hastie
Wireless Operator / Air Gunner

29th September 1940

When not on operations, bomber crews still faced mortal danger during training flights and night flying could prove particularly perilous. It was on such a night training flight that the crew of a 49 Squadron Hampden P2134 perished.

At 11:30pm on 29th September 1940 Sergeant Catley's aircraft was seen at Haigh near Wakefield in Yorkshire. Witnesses saw the Hampden in a turn at approximately one thousand feet. Shortly afterwards it flew into high ground and crashed. All three of the crew were killed. Over the years, some doubt has existed as to whether the aircraft had in fact crashed here or at Haigh in Lancashire.

Whilst researching this crash, various documents including the accident report, confirmed the location to be Haigh near Wakefield. Sergeant Catley was from Eynesford in Kent and Sergeant Hastie from Canvey Island in Essex. Both were 21 years of age. The third member of the crew, Sergeant William (Bill) Nichol, who was also a pilot, flying that night as navigator, is buried in Ayr Cemetery.

Hampden over Lincolnshire

Sergeant John Henry Green
Wireless Operator
Sergeant Basil Edward Redgrove
Pilot

3rd November 1940

Following repair or maintenance and before being classed as ready for operations an aircraft would need to be air tested. The idea of this test was to ensure that all engineering works had been carried out to the pilot's satisfaction and the aircraft was fit to fly. It was also customary to take a member of the ground crew who had worked on the aircraft on the flight. This was a real test of the faith of the engineers in the quality of their work.

On 3rd November 1940, such a test was to be carried out on Hampden X2978 of 83 Squadron at Scampton. The aircraft was flown by Sergeant Redgrove with his wireless operator Sergeant Green. Eighteen year old Aircraftman Second Class Robert Rowlands was also on the flight and although his role is unclear it is likely that he was the engineer to fly with the crew that day.

Whether it was a mechanical problem or not isn't known, but at 1pm the aircraft crashed seven miles south east of Retford in Nottinghamshire. The aircraft had hit a tree whilst flying at low level, killing all three of the crew on board. Robert Rowlands is buried in St Helens Cemetery.

Sergeant Ronald Norris
Wireless Operator /Air Gunner

4th November 1940

The war in Europe had been raging for just over a year, but Flying Officer Clare Arthur Connor was already a famous bomber pilot. On 4th November 1940 he was flying in command of an 83 Squadron Hampden number L4093. His target was Kiel in Germany; it was to be his and his crew's last flight.

Only two months previously Connor, together with his Air Gunner, Sergeant John Hannah, had successfully brought their crippled Hampden back from a raid to destroy German Invasion barges. On their second run on the target their aircraft was badly hit by flak and immediately caught fire. Such was the intensity of the blaze that

Sgt John Hannah VC

both the navigator and the under-gunner felt the aircraft was doomed and baled out immediately. Sergeant Hannah meanwhile fought to save the aircraft, using his bare hands to extinguish the flames.

For their courage, Sergeant Hannah received the Victoria Cross and Pilot Officer Connor the Distinguished Flying Cross. Sergeant Hannah took months to recover from his injuries, but he did eventually return to service as an air gunnery instructor. Although he survived the war, he never fully recovered from his injuries, dying of Tuberculosis at the age of 25 in June 1947.

At the entrance to Scampton churchyard, a small rose garden and memorial plaque pays tribute to this man's courage. The roses in the garden are crimson, the colour of the ribbon of the Victoria Cross.

Less than a month after Hannah received his Victoria Cross and Connor his DFC from His Majesty the King at Buckingham Palace, Flying Officer Connor and his replacement crew of three were departing on this new mission. At 5 am his aircraft was hit by flak and Connor set course for home. Only a few miles from the relative safety of land his aircraft crashed into the sea, just off Spurn Point, at the mouth of the River Humber.

The bodies of Sergeant James William Gibson and Sergeant Geoffrey Stubbings were never found and they are commemorated on the Runnymede Memorial. The bodies of Sergeant Norris and Pilot Officer Connor were washed ashore and afforded a military burial. Sergeant Norris is buried at Scampton and Pilot Officer Connor in Brattleby Church, the next village to Scampton.

Sgt Hannah (centre) recovering

Flying Officer Kenneth William Michie
Pilot
Sergeant Garton Vincent Davenport-Jones
Wireless Operator Air Gunner

8th December 1940

Sgt Davenport-Jones

On 7th December 1940 Hampden S for Sugar of 49 Squadron was one of a mixed force of forty five Blenheim, Whitley and Hampden aircraft that took-off from various stations to attack airfields in occupied Europe. Only a few months earlier, the Battle of Britain had been won by the narrowest of margins and this raid would have been one of many to ensure that the Luftwaffe were kept on the back-foot.

Just after midnight, 49 Squadron's aircraft were returning to Scampton, but S for Sugar came to grief only a couple of miles from home and safety. Whilst in the circuit, the aircraft went out of control and crashed. We will never know what happened to cause the pilot to lose control, but fatigue after a stressful mission may well have played a part. Three of the four crew on board were killed. As well as those buried at Scampton, Sergeant Thomas Goldie, was buried in Lesmahagow Cemetery in Lanarkshire. Miraculously, although very badly injured, Sergeant Barrier, a pilot acting in the capacity of Navigator on the flight survived.

Sergeant Peter Charles Prosser
Wireless Operator

12th January 1941

Hampden L4045 of 49 Squadron was a real survivor, up until the fateful night of 11th / 12th January 1941. It had completed just less than 800 hours of operational flying, a truly remarkable figure at the time.

The target for tonight was an important one. The Tirpitz was one of a new breed, one of Hitler's much-vaunted Pocket Battleships. The ship had awesome fighting statistics, displacing 42,900 tons with an overall length of 792 feet, it had a maximum speed of 30 knots and a range of 9,000 miles at 19 knots. With 2400 crew she was fast, manoeuvrable and heavily armed. Should she be allowed into the Atlantic, the Tirpitz would cause total carnage amongst the ships bringing vitally needed war materials from America.

RAF Intelligence suspected that the Tirpitz, sister ship of the infamous Bismarck, was at anchor in Wilhelmshaven harbour and 49 Squadron were ordered to dispatch nine aircraft to locate and attack it. On arrival over the target area the bombers found more extensive cloud cover than had been expected and only two aircraft were able to attack the ship itself; the remainder were only able to bomb the general harbour area. Unsurprisingly the Tirpitz survived the attack and was only destroyed nearly 4 years later. Having never made it to the Atlantic, the Tirpitz was at anchor in a Norwegian Fjord when it was eventually sunk by Lancasters of 9 and 617 Squadrons, using Barnes Wallis's 12,000 pound Tallboy bomb, the second most powerful bomb of World War 2.

49 Squadron pre flight briefing

For Pilot Officer Hugh Newhouse and his three crew members that night the seven hour mission was nearing its end. Over England and with the perils of German flak far behind them, their thoughts must surely have turned to breakfast and the highly prized egg that all bomber crews were entitled to after an   operational mission.

Nobody will ever know why the aircraft was flying so low, but overhead Northorpe in Lincolnshire, the pilot must have realised at the last moment that he was in serious danger.   Witnesses saw the aircraft pull up steeply to avoid houses; unfortunately this last desperate attempt to avoid disaster also caused the pilot to lose control and crash.   As well as nineteen-year-old Sergeant Prosser who is buried at Scampton, the remainder of the crew, Pilot Officer Newhouse, Sergeant Henry Irving the Navigator and Sergeant Leonard Jackson the air gunner were all killed.   They are buried at St Mary's Churchyard, Buckland, St Nicholas Cemetery, Newcastle and St Mary's Churchyard Prestwich respectively.

Wing Commander William Waters Stainthorpe AFC
Pilot

27th February 1941

The raid to Cologne was a big one for its time. On the night of 26th February 1941 a total of 126 aircraft were ordered to destroy two targets within the city. The officer commanding 83 Squadron, Wing Commander Stainthorpe, was flying as the pilot of Hampden X3124.

Despite ineffective flak over the target, the cost to Bomber Command that night would be high, losing two of its squadron commanders in just thirty minutes. Thirty year-old Wing Commander Stainthorpe from Guisborough was leading nine Hampden aircraft from his Squadron and upon finding the target in an area of good visibility; he must have thought that the bombing results would be very good.   With the mission accomplished, the crew turned westward for home and Safety.

Since the force had left Scampton at 9:50pm the weather had deteriorated badly and by the early hours of the following morning, as the bomber force was returning, there was a thick overcast with rain and snow below it.

Now lost and low on fuel, the crew of X3124 had one last hope; the RAF operated a system code-named Darky". This system utilised a network of short-range radio transmitters on a common frequency. A lost pilot could transmit on this frequency and each receiving station would get a bearing. If several stations received the transmission, the aircraft's position could be triangulated and radioed back to the pilot.

At 1:20am on 27th February the Darky station at Neston, achieved a fix on the aircraft putting it 15 miles south east of Birmingham.

However, this last lifeline came too late, as radio contact was lost before the fix could be passed. Just ten minutes later the Hampden smashed into high ground at Derrington Cross near Stafford, killing the entire crew.

Although Wing Commander Stainthorpe was an experienced pilot, with 2400 flying hours, it was subsequently found that this had been only his second night flight in a

Hampdens at Scampton

Hampden. Investigators at the time concluded that his inexperience on the type possibly contributed to the cause of the accident. William had originally gained his civilian pilot's licence at Newcastle Aero Club in 1929. He was awarded pilot's licence number 8490 by the Royal Aeronautical Club, the relatively low number reflecting just what an elite band pilots were in the early days of aviation.

Also killed were Pilot Officer Andrew Melville, Sergeant Leslie Emmerson, and Sergeant Douglas Weaving. They are buried at Chesham Burial Ground, Buckinghamshire, Acklam Cemetery, Middlesbrough and East Finchley Cemetery, London respectively. Just two weeks earlier Weaving had experienced a close call, in the same area when his aircraft collided with a barrage balloon cable. The aircraft was badly damaged, but the crew were able to bale out, giving Sergeant Weaving a very short reprieve from paying the ultimate sacrifice.

The other squadron commander lost that night, on the same raid, was Wing Commander Gerald Thomas Toland, the Officer Commanding 78 Squadron who, like Stainthorpe, was also 30 years old. His Whitley aircraft had taken off from Dishforth in North Yorkshire and had also successfully returned from its mission. Just 30 minutes after Stainthorpe had died Toland's aircraft crashed in the Scottish Highlands in very similar circumstances. He is buried at St Bartholomew Churchyard, Moreton Corbet, Shropshire.

Was the raid worth it? Well, just 10 high explosive bombs and 90 incendiaries fell on the city of Cologne that night. In other words, just under 3% of the high explosive bombs and 0.6% of incendiaries dropped hit the entire city. It is not known if any at all hit the intended targets within the city. Had Bomber Command known these figures in advance, it would seem likely that they would have reconsidered the raid. It must be remembered though, that at this time of the war Bomber Command were virtually this country's only means of taking the war to the enemy. In this sense, the raid had enormous value; technical developments later in the war would bring the required accuracy.

Pilot Officer Leslie Richard Evans
Pilot/Navigator

4th April 1941

Gardening was the code-name given to the RAF's efforts to mine German sea-lanes. The areas to be mined were given further code-names in the forms of vegetables, plants and flowers. Gardening for cinnamon for example would decode to mean conduct mine laying operations off La Rochelle. With just such a mission, on 3rd April 1941 Flight Lieutenant Reginald Thompson led his crew towards the French coast in an 83 Squadron Hampden, number AD 748.

Mining was a complex and dangerous operation. The crew would first have to locate a pre-selected landmark on the enemy coast. From there they would have to

A Naval Petty Officer at Scampton supervises the arming of anti ship mines prior to a Gardening mission

fly a timed leg on a precise heading. Increasing their vulnerability still further, they also needed to slow to 200 miles per hour, so that the mine did not disintegrate on impact with the sea. Only once all of this was achieved, could a mine be placed accurately enough to do the required damage to German shipping.

With his mine successfully placed in the shipping channels off La Rochelle, Thompson and the other 14 Hampdens on this mission headed for home. Since their 6:45pm take-off from Scampton however, fog had enveloped much of England and a diversion to another airfield became necessary.

At least three Hampdens including Thompson's, selected St Eval in Cornwall as their diversion airfield. Two aircraft crashed on or close to the airfield, without casualties, but Hampden AD 748 was never destined to land there. At 2:10am the next day, the 19 Group controller reported the crash of an aircraft which had last been fixed overhead Lizard.

At first light Lysander aircraft were dispatched to search for the wreckage and any possible survivors. Sadly there were no survivors to be found. The aircraft had crashed into the 1948 ft high peak of Hangingstone Hill on Dartmoor killing all on board. Although the cause of the crash has never been determined for certain, there was speculation that the pilot or navigator mistook the height of the peak, represented on the map in metres, for feet. This would have led the crew to believe that the high ground was well below them as they continued to search for their diversion airfield.

Pilot Officer Evans had been keen to join the Royal Air Force and had gained his Private Pilot's Licence on 26th August 1939 to aid him in this ambition. By the 7th September 1939 he had achieved his aim and joined in the rank of Acting Pilot Officer. A year later, he was made a substantive Pilot Officer and by March 1941 had commenced flying duties with 83 Squadron at Scampton.

Sadly he was only to spend four weeks with 83 Squadron before the fatal crash in which he was acting as Navigator.

Leslie and Phyllis on their wedding day

Before the war, Leslie Evans had trained as an engineer at His Majesty's Dockyard Colleges at Portsmouth and Bermuda. After training, he worked for the Burmah Oil Company until the war broke out. In February 1940 he married his wife Phyllis and at the time of the crash they were expecting their first child. Leslie had promised his wife Phyllis that whatever else happened he would be present at the birth.

A little over 24 hours after the crash, Phyllis was in a nursing home near Lincoln Cathedral giving birth to their son Richard. Phyllis was not aware that her husband had died, but during the birth she had a very clear vision of him. It would seem that Leslie was determined to keep his promise.

Flight Lieutenant Thompson, who hailed from Boars Hill in Oxfordshire, is buried in his home county at St Leonard's Churchyard in Sunningwell. He had attended University and gained a Bachelor of Arts Degree (Oxon).

The other crew members who died were Sergeant Leslie Eden who lies buried in Camberwell New Cemetery Southwark and Sergeant Alan Murray who is buried in Exeter Higher Cemetery.

Leutnant Kurt Hanning
Pilot
Unteroffizier Wilhelm A C Hansen
Gerfreiter Johannes Dietrich
Gerfreiter E H Reidel
Gerfreiter Helmuth Wimmeder

12th May 1941

Helmuth Wimmeder

Throughout World War 2 the Germans launched many bombing raids against RAF airfields and Scampton did not escape the attention of the Luftwaffe. On this occasion Luftflotte 3 had sent 240 aircraft from Denmark, to attack various airfields in England. Kurt Hanning and his crew had left Griefwald on the Baltic with Lincolnshire's bomber bases firmly in their sights. Their aircraft was a Junkers JU88, painted green with distinctive red spinners on the propellers.

At 01:35am on 12th May 1941 they began their attack on Scampton airfield, hoping to wreak havoc with the aircraft's full war-load of twenty eight 50 kilogram bombs. They had already made several low passes over the airfield when they made the mistake of over-flying Corporal Inkpen and his 6-man gun crew.

Cpl Inkpen's crew opened up with two Lewis guns and expended all their ammunition on the target. Grievous damage was caused to the aircraft, and it burst into flames crashing close to the airfield boundary near Brattleby Lane.

In the midst of all this drama, Mr Miller, the Station's Rolls Royce Representative and his wife were driving along the Scampton to Ingham Road. Seeing the bomber crash he rushed to the burning wreckage hoping to rescue the crew. He succeeded in pulling Kurt Hanning from the wreckage alive. However, Hanning was badly injured having received several bullet wounds and died in Mrs Miller's arms only five minutes later. In the mean time, Mr Miller returned to the bomber and rescued three more of the crew, but they were all either dead or very quickly succumbed to their wounds. Scampton personnel buried Hanning, Hansen, Dietrich and Wimmeder with full military honours on the 14th May 1941.

The tail of the aircraft was recovered the next day and inscribed with Corporal Inkpen's name and subsequently kept by 83 Squadron as a trophy.

Sadly, just over three months later, Corporal Inkpen was himself killed when a Hampden returning from operations blew up on the dispersal where he was working.

Above and below: Damage caused to Scampton's Armoury during the raid

It was not until years later that the remains of Gerfreiter Reidel were discovered at the site of the crash by a farmer who was ploughing the field. It would seem that he was a member of the ground crew and that he had persuaded the pilot to take him along to experience the war first hand. Strictly against regulations, the crew would have been careful to ensure that nobody noticed him being snuck aboard the aircraft. With the Luftwaffe unaware that he was aboard that aircraft, his disappearance must have been a great mystery for many years. Once found, Reidel was buried in the same grave as Wimmeder, thus explaining the two names on the one grave marker in the churchyard.

There are many local rumours surrounding this crash, all of which have proven difficult to verify. Some say that Gerfreiter Reidel was in fact a woman and the pilot's girlfriend. Other reports state that there was a small riot in the village, before the Germans were buried, in which the vicarage was pelted with stones. The fact that the locals were vehemently opposed to the enemy being buried in their churchyard is perhaps understandable when it is seen against the losses we were suffering at the time and the almost constant bombing raids on Lincolnshire. Whatever the truth of these rumours, the crew now lie buried in well tended graves which are cared for by the village.

The German crew are buried with Full Military Honours.

Aircraftman 2nd Class Michael Fraser Cross
Aircraftman 2nd Class John Metcalfe

21st May 1941

Eighteen year old Michael Cross was the son of Major Charles Cross, an officer in the Royal Artillery. Michael was originally from Church Stretton in Shropshire. He, along with John Metcalfe, aged 20, were killed in what should have been a routine transit flight to Dunholme Lodge, an airfield within easy walking distance of Scampton. The pressure to get pilots to the frontline quickly often meant that they arrived on squadrons with very little training. 83 Squadron was no exception. On 21st May 1941 the pilot of Hampden AD898 was Sergeant Olaf Nicholas Stromberg. He had a total of only sixty three hours as a solo pilot and by the time of the accident, he had accrued just ten hours on the Hampden.

In what was thought to be a combination of over-confidence and inexperience, immediately after take-off Stromberg attempted a steep turn without waiting for sufficient speed to do so. To compound his problems he also failed to raise the under-carriage and produced yet more drag. The stall that followed would have seemed all too inevitable to the more experienced pilots watching the disaster unfold. Recovery from a stall at low level would have been virtually impossible, even for a very experienced pilot. The aircraft crashed killing all three on board. Sergeant Stromberg is buried in Portobello Cemetery Edinburgh, the town of his birth.

Pilot Officer Ernest Rene Davis
Pilot

14th August 1941

The Hampden was beginning to take its toll on the RAF crews that flew it, not only on operations but also in training. This fact cannot have escaped the senior officers at Scampton and any perceived flying indiscipline that could lead to even more casualties would have been dealt with severely. However, the temptation to demonstrate your new found flying skills to family members sometimes proved too strong for some pilots to resist, often with devastating consequences.

At 8:20pm on 13th August 1941, 83 Squadron Hampden AD935 took-off on a local night flying test with Pilot Officer Davis at the controls. A little more than four hours later at 12:40am on 14th, with the test presumably completed, Pilot Officer Davis succumbed to the temptation to fly low over the house where his wife was staying.

As he made his low-level approach to the house in Evesham, the aircraft struck tree and crashed. Davis and Sergeant Gilbert Newbold, also a pilot, were killed. Newbold, just 21 years old is buried in Sileby Cemetery in Leicestershire. Miraculously, Sergeant W. Wells the third crew member survived but was injured.

On the accident report, both the Air Officer Commanding and the Station Commander made the feelings on the matter clear and made the following remark. "Regulations have again been brought forcibly to the notice of all crews".

Sergeant William Thomas Ross Stephenson
Pilot
Pilot Officer Patrick Joseph Murphy
Air Gunner
Flight Sergeant Stanley Charles Steward
Observer

16th August 1941

Not all the burials here relate to Scampton based aircraft. During the war, if an aircraft belonging to another unit crashed within Scampton's area of responsibility, it was the station's duty to organise the burials. At 23:27 Wellington W5532 took-off from RAF Driffield in East Yorkshire as part of a force of 72 aircraft attacking Cologne. Only minutes later, this 104 Squadron aircraft crashed at South Leverton, killing all on board. Further casualties were narrowly avoided when the aircraft's bomb load exploded. PC Hollingsworth, of East Retford Police Station witnessed the entire event, his Police report follows:

"At 0001hrs on the night of 16th/17th August 1941 I heard machine gun fire to the North East of South Leverton and observed tracer bullets. A minute later I observed an aircraft falling in flames. At 0002 hrs I heard the aircraft hit the ground and explode. I proceeded to the spot as quickly as possible and took charge. I was unable to approach the burning aircraft owing to the fierce heat of the fire. However, I remained in close proximity. At 0030 hrs there was a terrific explosion caused by the bombs exploding and I was hurled seventy yards by the blast. I suffered no serious injury."

This can be seen as a reliable account of events and gives rise to the possibility that W5532 was shot down. It is by no means certain that this was due to enemy action. What is now known as blue-on-blue was extremely common during World War II. The only way of determining friend from foe was visual identification by the fighter pilot. Although it was not uncommon for friendly aircraft to be engaged in broad daylight, the problem was much worse at night. Throughout the war, the Luftwaffe were mostly

Hans Hahn

equipped with twin engine bombers, and it is possible that an RAF pilot mistook the twin engine Wellington for a German bomber.

However, on this night one of the Luftwaffe's night-fighter aces was on the prowl over Lincolnshire. After the war, it was found that Lieutenant Hans Hahn, had made a claim for a Wellington shot down in the Scunthorpe area. As no other Wellington was lost over the United Kingdom that night, it would seem likely that it was in fact the same aircraft. This was Hans Hahn's 11th victory, but his next would also claim his own life. Less than two months later he died when his Ju88 collided with the twin-engine Oxford he was attacking over Grantham.

The Pilot of the Wellington was a member of the Royal Canadian Air Force and because of the Canadian Government's enlightened attitude towards the release of personnel records we know a little more about this man. Sergeant Stephenson had previously served as a Private in the Canadian Army and in peace time had run his own business as the owner and manager of a flour mill in Omemee, Ontario.

Transferring to the RCAF on the 1st June 1940, Thomas listed his hobbies as Hockey, Softball, Golf, Swimming, Skiing and Tennis. It is possible that, like many aircrew volunteers, that he had ambitions of becoming a fighter pilot. Under the section entitled Hobbies useful to the RCAF he lists Hunting. At the time, skills acquired such as hunting were thought to be extremely useful to a fighter pilot.

Whatever his ambitions though, Thomas was selected as a Bomber Pilot and after basic flying training in Canada, he shipped out to the UK on the 28th February 1941. Completing his flying training on 19 Operational Training Unit at RAF Kinloss, he was then posted to active duty on 104 Squadron on the 6th May of the same year.

Also killed: Sergeant John Walter Nowlan (pilot), buried in Eltham Churchyard Southwark. Sergeant Kenneth Hutchinson (Wireless Operator), buried in Long Eaton Cemetery, Derbyshire and Sergeant Ivor Howard Arthur Henderson, buried in Chickerell Churchyard in Dorset.

Pilot Officer Victor Charles Ormond Maybury
Pilot

25th August 1941

By now, Scampton was no stranger to tragedy but the early hours of the 25th August 1941 were to prove particularly harrowing.   Despite all the aircraft returning safely from the target, the operation that night to Dusseldorf would cost the lives of sixteen Scampton personnel on or close to the airfield.

AE223 was one of six Hampdens that had been sent to Wesel for searchlight suppression duties. This was a dangerous but vital mission, the aim of which was to attack active searchlights with small bombs and machine guns.

The effect of these attacks was quickly evident. It was found that not only did the searchlight usually lose its target, but also that within 25 minutes of the start of these attacks nearly all searchlight activity in the area could be thwarted.

For bomber crews, their greatest fear was being caught by a searchlight, for once illuminated, and losing the cover of darkness, every gunner in the area homed-in on them. No doubt the work of the searchlight suppression crews was greatly appreciated.

Upon returning from operations it was normal procedure for an aircraft to taxi to dispersal, shut-down its engines and open the bomb-bay doors so that the ground crew could check for hung-up bombs. Un-beknown to the pilot of AE223, twenty two year old Pilot Officer Maybury, he had indeed experienced a hang-up, but this one was particularly nasty.

The aircraft had returned with at least one bomb hung up which at some point had fallen into the closed bomb bay. As they shut down their engines and taxied to the dispersal the bomb-bay doors were opened so that the armourers could check the bomb bay. At this point the bomb fell to the floor and exploded, killing the entire crew as well as four of the ground crew gathered nearby. One of the unfortunate ground crew was Corporal William Inkpen, who had shot down the Junkers 88 mentioned earlier in the book.

Apart from Pilot Officer Maybury, who was buried at Scampton, the following 83 Squadron aircrew were returned home for burial. Pilot Officer Thomas MacIntyre is buried in Eastwood Cemetery, Glasgow. Twenty two year old Sergeant Edward Clarke, buried in Woodgrange Park Cemetery, East Ham and Sergeant Ronald Scholes, buried in Audenshaw Cemetery, Lancashire.

The 16 aircrew around this Hampden gives some impression of the loss of life that night

42

The four 83 Squadron ground crew killed also went home for burial. Corporal William Inkpen is buried in St Mary's New Churchyard, Old Basing, Hampshire, Leading Aircraftman Leonard Rayment is buried in Camberwell New Cemetery, Southwark, Aircraftman First Class William Stevenson, is buried in All Saints Churchyard near Manchester and twenty three year old Aircraftman 2nd Class Colin Ogden is interred in Stockport Crematorium.

Flight Lieutenant Anthony John Mills DFC
Pilot
Sergeant Bernard Victor Mason
Wireless Operator / Air Gunner
Sergeant Owen Bernard McMahon
Pilot

25th August 1941

With eight dead already, few at Scampton could have suspected that the night was going to get much worse. Just twenty five minutes later however, it did, when Hampdens X3121 of 83 Squadron and AD967 of 49 Squadron collided on final approach to the airfield. Both these aircraft had been on a mission to Dusseldorf.

Over sixty years later, the reasons for the collision can only be speculated upon. However, the burning wreckage of AE223 must, at the very least, have been a severe distraction. It is possible that those still airborne believed that the burning aircraft were the result of an attack by a German intruder. Taking action to save themselves from the same fate, both crews would have sought the cover of darkness. It is known that both aircraft had turned off their navigation lights, but as well as gaining cover from enemy intruders, they had inadvertently made themselves virtually impossible to see in time to avoid a collision in the busy airspace over Scampton.

The wreckage of the two bombers fell on Whale Jaws Farm on the north eastern boundary of the airfield. All eight aircrew were killed. Two of the crew of the 83 Squadron aircraft, Mason and Mills and one of the 49 Squadron crew, McMahon are buried at Scampton. The rest were returned home for burial.

From AD967 of 49 Squadron, Sergeant Ernest Welbourne is buried in the Arnold Cemetery Nottingham and Sergeant Ian MacKinnon is buried in Brookwood Military Cemetery, near London. For whatever reasons, MacKinnon was not taken back to his parental home in Dundee.

The twenty three year old Pilot / Navigator Sergeant Gathorne Upton is buried in Bandon Hill Cemetery Surrey. From X3121 of 83 Squadron Sergeant John Somerville is buried in Largo Cemetery, Leven in Scotland and Flight Sergeant Donald Sharp is buried in Portslade Cemetery, Brighton.

43

Sergeant Thomas Haydon Smith
Pilot

29th September 1941

On 28th September 1941, 49 Sqn had tasked fourteen of its aircraft for a small attack against Frankfurt, but their efforts were to be frustrated from the start. Four aircraft were scrubbed from the mission before take-off and a fifth suffered a tail wheel collapse, also removing it from the mission.

The 29th September was only eleven minutes old when Sergeant Smith's Hampden AE376, one of those that did get airborne, entered a shallow dive and crashed on the Burton Estate just north of Lincoln. The reason for this crash is unknown.

All on board were killed. Sergeant Alfred Walker is buried at Hunstanton Cemetery Sussex, Sergeant Albert Raine is buried in St Mary's Churchyard, Howden le Wear, Durham and Sergeant Reginald Greenhalgh is commemorated in Manchester Crematorium.

In addition to this the squadron lost another aircraft and crew over enemy territory that night. Fortunately, they were all able to escape their aircraft and were taken prisoner of war.

Sergeant Thomas Hollas Hardisty
Wireless Operator

8th December 1941

On the 8th December 1941, Hampden AE227 of 49 Squadron was on a routine training exercise flying in the local area when its Wireless Operator, Sergeant Hardisty mysteriously fell from or baled out of the aircraft. Unfortunately although he was wearing his parachute it did not open. Welton Police later found his body in the Sudbrooke area.

A 49 Squadron Hampden similar to the one Hardisty was in

Occurrences such as this were not as uncommon as one might imagine. In their isolated position within the aircraft, an intercom lead might become disconnected. If this was followed by a sudden or unexpected manoeuvre, the crew member would contact the pilot to find out what was happening. Due to the disconnected lead, his question would be met with silence, it might then be reasonable to assume the rest of the crew had baled-out and following suit would seem very sensible.

In this case, the pilot, Pilot Officer Andrews was practicing formation flying and whilst changing formation, he had to turn suddenly to avoid another aircraft. In doing so, the aircraft entered a condition known as stabilised yaw. This was a well-known flaw in the Hampden's design and caused the aircraft to stall and lose height rapidly. Although the pilot subsequently stated that he never feared for the safety of the aircraft, he was only able to recover it to normal flight at 100 feet. If Sergeant Hardisty had bailed-out at this height, believing the aircraft was about to crash, he would not have had time to open his parachute, before he hit the ground.

Sergeant Lloyd Donald James Crozier RCAF
Pilot
Sergeant Thomas Dunbar Dakin RCAF
Pilot

23rd March 1942

1518 Beam Approach Training Flight was based at Scampton and used Airspeed Oxford aircraft to train and refresh pilots in the use of the Beam Approach Beacon System (BABS). This system allowed pilots to land in bad weather when the runway was not visible.

A beacon was placed at the end of the runway in use, which sent out either dots or dashes depending on whether the pilot was left, or right of the runway. The pilot could then fly the aircraft towards the centre line of the runway and as he descended out of the very low cloud, the runway should be right in front of him ready to land on.

On 23rd March 1942, under the guidance of their instructor Flying Officer Hugh McGuffie, two Canadian pilots, Sergeant Dakin and Sergeant Crozier were practicing such approaches at Dunholme

Airspeed Oxford

Cockpit of the Oxford

Lodge, when at 2:40pm their aircraft AT659 struck power lines and crashed at Pickering's Farm, to the south of the airfield. All three were killed.

The pilot had been ordered to conduct the flight at 2000 feet and just 10 minutes prior to the crash, the Squadron Commander himself had seen the aircraft at the correct height. The reason why the aircraft subsequently descended has always remained a mystery.

Donald Crozier, had joined the Royal Canadian Air Force on 13th May 1941. He originally came from Carndruff, Saskatchewan where he was employed as a truck driver. He was an enthusiastic sportsman and played hockey and basketball as well as being a keen swimmer who had previously been employed as a Life Guard for two years. Having completed his flying training in Canada and having been awarded his pilot's wings on the 19th December 1941, he arrived in the United Kingdom in January 1942.

Thomas Dunbar, the other student onboard, had arrived in the country the same day as Crozier. He was originally from Regina in Saskatchewan, where he had studied at the University of Saskatchewan's Regina College. He abandoned his studies after a year to join the Royal Canadian Air Force on the 15th April 1941. This must have been a difficult decision, especially as his father, who was a Surgeon, may well have expected him to complete his studies.

The two students were buried at Scampton, a place they had not had time to learn a great deal about and such a very long way from home. The instructor, Flying Officer McGuffie, is buried at St John's Churchyard, Taxal, Derbyshire. The inquest held at Scampton on the 25th of March 1942 reached a verdict of Accidental Death.

With so much flying going on it is important to remember those behind the scenes. Above left Scampton's Flying Control and right the Station Telephone Exchange

Pilot Officer William Henry Parr
Pilot
Flight Sergeant Kenneth Gilbert McKee
Wireless Operator / Air Gunner
Flight Sergeant David Charles MacNab
Air Observer

16th May 1942

The role of 16 Operational Training Unit (OTU) at Upwood was to take aircrew from basic flying training and convert them onto their first operational aircraft type, in this case the Hampden.   The necessity of getting aircrew to the frontline inevitably meant that training was not as thorough as might be expected in peacetime.

To a newly qualified pilot, flying on instruments in the dark could be an extremely daunting prospect. For twenty five year old William Parr, this seems to have been a particular problem, as shortly before this accident he had been to see his Station Commander expressing doubts in his own ability.

The Station Commander reassured him that there was no reason to be troubled and he should continue with his night flying training.

Just before midnight on the 16th May 1942, Parr and his crew were on a night navigation exercise from Upwood. At 4000 feet, they encountered cloud and decided to climb above it. As William Parr climbed his aircraft to 10,000 feet, he must have allowed his speed to reduce. It was at this point that he lost control of his Hampden and it entered a spin.

One of the air gunners managed to fit his parachute and escape in time. The rest of the crew however, were prevented from reaching their parachutes by the massive forces being exerted upon them as a result of the aircraft spinning. At one minute to midnight their Hampden number P2120 crashed near Saxilby in Lincolnshire, killing the three remaining crew members. Parr's fears had been fully justified.

Hampden at Scampton. This one is believed to be the first to arrive at the station.

As a result of this accident, the Officer Commanding 16 OTU re-briefed all his crews and impressed upon them the need to wear parachutes whilst flying in cloud.

Flight Sergeant McKee had joined the Royal Canadian Air Force on the 14th September 1940. Originally from Ingersoll, Ontario, before the war Kenneth had been a machinist. He was an extremely motivated person who listed his reason for joining the RCAF as follows, "I believe it is my duty to my King and country to do all I can to help win the war. It is my opinion that this can best be accomplished as a member of the RCAF".

Flight Sergeant MacNab, another Canadian, was from Windsor, Ontario. He had worked as a bottle washer and also as an usher at the Capitol Theatre in Windsor, before he gained employment as a stockman for the Ford Motor Company. He worked there until joining the RCAF on 6th January 1941. His parents also lived in Windsor where his father was the Chief of Detectives for the Windsor Police Department.

It appears that David initially trained as a pilot, but did not pass the course. Not letting this deter him, he immediately went on to train as an Observer. The name of the surviving Air Gunner was Sergeant N D Mullins of the Royal Canadian Air Force.

Pilot Officer Leicester Bond Ware
Pilot

26th May 1942

A modern day picture of a Spitfire

An extremely popular member of 616 Squadron, twenty six year old New Zealander, Leicester Bond Ware was known to all as Tess. On 6th May 1942, he was flying his Spitfire VI number BR 172 against another aircraft from 303 (Poznan) Squadron of the Polish Air Force.

Tess had taken-off from Kings Cliffe near Peterborough and the Polish aircraft from Kirton in Lindsey to carry out practice intercepts with each other. At some point during this sortie, Bond's aircraft was seen to dive at great speed, before breaking up and crashing at Dunholme. The speed of the dive would have made escape from the aircraft virtually impossible and he died in the resultant impact.

Kings Cliffe became a USAF base in 1943 and it was where Major Glenn Miller conducted his last Hangar Concert on 3rd October 1944 before he disappeared on December 15th 1944 over the English Channel on a flight to Paris.

Sergeant Kenneth Aird
Sergeant George Lawson Mustoe
Sergeant Roy George Peverill

30th May 1942

By this time in the war, Bomber Harris, the Air Officer Commanding in Chief of Bomber Command knew that his policy of a strategic bombing campaign was in jeopardy. So far Bomber Command had not managed to get enough bombs on target to achieve the war winning results Harris desired. What was required was a demonstration of the effects of concentrated air power over a single target. In order to achieve the concentration that Harris needed, one thousand bombers would be required to stream over a single target in just 90 minutes.

The first problem he faced was that there were only 400 operationally ready aircraft and crews on his strength. To plug the shortfall, aircraft from training units, operational conversion units and even Coastal Command were co-opted into the mission. In a number of cases partially trained crews were also tasked to take part.

Cologne was selected as the first German city to see the effects of 1000 heavy bombers. In the words of Air Marshal Harris "The Nazis entered this war under the rather childish delusion that they were going to bomb everyone else and nobody was going to bomb them. At Rotterdam, London, Warsaw, and half a dozen other places they put their rather naive theory into operation. They sowed the wind, and now they are going to reap the whirlwind"

150 Squadron at Snaith in Yorkshire took their part in what was to become a highly significant, but costly mission. X3448 was a Vickers Wellington III twin engine bomber, the ingenious work of Dr Barnes Wallace a man whose fame would later become forever tied to Scampton and the "Dambusters".

Sergeant Aird and his crew took-off at 11:15pm on the 29th May 1942 as part of the first thousand bomber raid. It would seem however that the aircraft had encountered some type of problem and was returning to base, for only 3 hours later it was back over England. At 2:15am the aircraft crashed at Mottram's Farm near Faldingworth in Lincolnshire. All six crew were killed instantly. Although the cause of the crash could not be ascertained for certain, it was thought that an engine may have suddenly failed, causing the pilot to lose control and enter a spin.

The raid itself destroyed 600 acres of Cologne and caused 5000 casualties. Despite the loss of 39 aircraft or 4% of the bomber force, the raid was considered a success, vindicating Harris' faith in strategic bombing. Winston Churchill said of the raid "This proof of the growing power of the British bomber force is also the herald of what Germany will receive, city by city, from now on"

The three crew members buried at Scampton are all Australian. Sergeant Aird was 33 years old and the son of Dr Ivie and Mrs Aird of Bondi Junction, New South Wales. Sergeant Mustoe was from Queensland and Sergeant Peverill was from Victoria. Also killed in the crash was Sergeant Stanley Shaw, the pilot, who is buried in Nunhead Cemetery, London, Sergeant Joachim Dean who is buried in Southborough Cemetery, Kent and Sergeant Leonard Beck who is buried in Manchester Cemetery.

Flight Lieutenant Charles Henry Butt
Pilot
Flying Officer Robert Simpson Shaw
Pilot

4th November 1942

On the 4th November 1942 the weather over Scampton was particularly poor, but none-the-less, a weather test was ordered to see if it was fit for flying. Twenty two year old Flight Lieutenant Charles Butt of 1518 Beam Approach Training Flight and his student, Flying Officer Robert Shaw, took-off from Scampton to complete this test. Weather flights usually include climbing through cloud to establish the cloud base and the weather above it. They were flying in an Airspeed Oxford number AT663.

An idea of how the Beam (originally called Blind) Approach Training Flight normally operated is given by trainee pilot of the time Leslie Landell:

> *"It was a most demanding course, taking some 2 weeks, weather permitting, mostly consisting of taking off up to 100 feet or so then the instructor pulled a screen over your side of the cockpit blacking out everything. From then on you flew by instruments only, guided by the radio beam system, until you were on the final stage of the approach for landing, when the instructor removed the screen." (Leslie Landell WW2 People's War).*

At some point in the air test, Charles Butt contacted the control tower and reported that he was having difficulty with the beam set. Knowing that he was now unable to make a safe approach into Scampton, the control tower, very sensibly, advised him to fly South where the weather was better, with both North Luffenham and Bircham Newton fit for landing visually. Despite this advice, he persisted in trying to land at Scampton. Over the years, the RAF has put a name to this type of misplaced determination, "Press-on-itis". In other words, continuing with your intended plan in the face of over whelming evidence that you shouldn't. It often ended in disaster.

The aircraft was heard flying overhead the airfield and two maroons were fired. It was next heard making an approach well off the runway centre line. At 2:30pm the inevitable happened when the wing of the Oxford hit trees and crashed at Grange Farm, Brattleby, killing both of them. The report into this accident is quite telling, the Station Commander leaving no doubt as to whom he felt was to blame:

"The primary cause of this accident was due to bad airmanship on the part of the pilot, in that he, in spite of being told over the R/T that there was a clearance in the weather to the South, persisted in attempting a landing at base, instead of proceeding in the direction of the better weather. In attempting a landing in very bad visibility the aircraft hit an obstruction and crashed, and both pilots were killed." A contributory cause may have been that the S.B.A. (Standard Beam Approach) set was u/s (Un-serviceable) in fact the pilot reported this as being the case. Even if the S.B.A. set had failed, this failure was in no way responsible for the subsequent calamity. The accident, in my opinion, was simply caused by an error of judgment on the part of the pilot who besides flying the aircraft in such a manner as to cause it to hit an obstruction, failed to take proper advantage of the advice he was offered from the ground, regarding alternative aerodromes where he could have landed safely. As the cause of the accident is, in my opinion, obvious, I do not propose to convene a court of enquiry or appoint an investigating officer, further enquiry will not serve any useful purpose and in addition, there are no lessons which can be learnt as a result of this accident."

Signed J.N.H. Whitworth G/Cpt
Scampton 8.11.42.

The Officer Commanding 1518 Flight added: *"This pilot was a very experienced Beam pilot in whom I had complete faith. It is beyond my comprehension why he came down so low as to hit the trees knowing the visibility was bad. Had he flown south he could have landed normally in good visibility."*

In retrospect, there may have been a rush to judgment in this case. There were so many accidents at this time that those investigating them did not have the luxury of dwelling too long on each. The faulty Beam Approach set does seem to be significant and perhaps whilst making the approach, the pilot felt that the problem had rectified itself, the faulty set could in fact have been giving him a false reading that led him to believe he was in fact safely on the approach.

One thing is for sure, had the same accident happened today, a great deal more investigation would have taken place. Flying Officer Shaw was a Canadian from Gainsborough Saskatchewan, who before the war was a farmer.

The following is an insight into Charles Butt's life as recalled by his younger brother Peter and kindly passed on by his nephew Graeme Young. Using extracts from Peter's memoirs gives a clear insight into Jim's family, his background and the times.

"Charles Henry, known to all as Jim was my immediate senior in the family. Because of the depression Jim had to leave school after the fourth form and had two unsatisfactory jobs, car painting and furniture polishing, before joining the borough council as a clerk (which he hated according to the family).

"Grandfather came from a well-established Gloucester family where he left at an early age and ran off to sea. Whether he committed a misdemeanour or not is not quite clear. He married in Australia before settling in Whangarei, New Zealand. Jim's father was the oldest of 10 children. He was self-taught and became a reporter for New Zealand's largest newspaper and later ran the Waikato branch based in Hamilton where they lived.

Jim was born in Thames, a small coastal town started during the gold rush. Jim attended Hamilton Technical College where he was in the 1st eleven and 1st fifteen. The

family didn't own a car during the depression, but father used to own a motor bike which he drove very sedately. On one occasion he returned without Jim who had been riding pillion. To mother's question "Where's Jim' he had no answer. Jim had been jolted off somewhere along the road, but was no worse for wear.

I was 17 when war broke out, and brother Jim decided to join the Air Force, tackling the assignments prior to being accepted. He was less a

The Hamilton Technical Old Boys' Colts 1939. In the Championship they played 15, won 15 with 221 points for and 66 points against. Charles Butt is front row second in from the right as viewed.

student than I, but of course had less schooling. He enlisted in the third war course of the RNZAF in 1940 and after attending the initial training wing at Levin, and the elementary flying training school at New Plymouth, was posted to Woodbourne, Blenheim where he flew Vincent Wildebeests.

No. 3C (War) Course. Woodbourne, 1941.

GORDON McUSKER   BLENHEIM

Back Row—A. G. Herbert Hamilton, F. W. Latchland Picton, A. B. Clark Auckland, I. J. McNeil Tiki Tiki, J. R. Court Auckland

2nd Row—C. S. V. Gordwin Auckland, D. P. S. Lee Nelson, D. G. A. Price Nelson, D. F. P. Jennings Wanganui, L. M. Ralph Auckland
P. R. C. Clark Auckland, A. O. Hawkins Auckland, C. J. Salt Hastings, C. H. Butt Hamilton

Front Row—H. K. Horne Blenheim, W. H. Massey Auckland, W. M. Golden Auckland, J. Fisher Auckland, D. M. Mackenzie Hamilton,
D. S. Hunter Lower Hutt, I. M. Field Nelson, D. A. Stevenson Nelson, G. D. Askew Gisborne

Receiving his flying brevet or "wings" he left New Zealand in 1941 and was posted to an operational training unit at Lossiemouth, Scotland, where he converted to Wellingtons. Attached to 57 squadron at Feltwell, Cambridge, he completed 10 bombing operations as a second pilot, before commanding the aircraft for a raid on Munster. This trip was aborted because an engine overheated, but there were many more.

On his 31st trip over enemy territory the aircraft was chased by an enemy night fighter, but managed to escape. His first tour over, Jim was posted as an instructor to No. 18 Blind Approach Flight at Scampton, five miles from the City of Lincoln. He was commissioned and eventually became a flight commander with the rank of Flight Lieutenant.

A highly competent navigator in foggy conditions, his competence was recognised by a recommendation for an Air force Cross. Assessed as an above average pilot in Blind Approach Systems he was expecting to return to operations. Before being posted to a squadron and receiving the recommended award, equipment failed as he was about to touch down and his aircraft hit a tree on the edge of the runway. His death was a tragic shock to my parents. It wasn't until she and my father visited the grave twenty years later that my mother finally accepted Jim's death. I attended his funeral at Scampton in 1942, and was privileged to make a pilgrimage to his grave in 1986. We were good friends, and his death affected us all.

Returning from a scramble at Bolt Head on November the 4th 1942, I was told by the Flight Commander, Dusty Miller (he was later killed) that my brother Jim had died in a flying accident at Scampton. I was shocked - Jim was a very experienced pilot.

Charles Butt

Our first meeting after my arrival in England was on a bus on my way out to Scampton to see him. I hadn't then known he had been commissioned, and I didn't recognise him immediately in his pilot officers uniform. We met on another occasion at Nottingham, where we stayed in the same hotel. I remember that night because I escorted a girl home from a dance without realising that we were travelling on the last bus. I had a long walk home.

Given leave to attend the funeral, I flew my Typhoon back to squadron headquarters at Exeter, and was allowed to take the Tiger Moth to Lincoln. With visibility down to a few hundred yards, I flew in murky conditions over the Midlands. I didn't realise I was over Coventry until I saw a large anti-aircraft balloon at the same level and not far from the line I was flying. After refuelling, I saw the tower at Lincoln Cathedral standing out of the fog, and was soon taxying alongside the Lancaster bombers used by Guy Gibson and 617 squadron on the raid to the Mohne Dam. They were stationed at Scampton and were recognisable by the fittings used to hold the mines designed to breached the Dams.

As Jim was by then a Flight Lieutenant, there was a significant attendance of brass hats, bands and airmen at the funeral. I don't remember meeting the padre but assume I did. Jim's colleagues were very supportive.

It was a lovely Sunday morning when I took off from Scampton and headed south. The petrol gauge in a Tiger Moth isn't easy to read from the back cockpit, but when I thought fuel was becoming low I landed on an aerodrome which turned out to be a maintenance unit. There was no one about on Sunday. I took off again in the knowledge that there were many aerodromes further south. I had just begun to traverse the Salisbury plains when the propeller stopped turning.

I had run out of petrol. It was all very embarrassing, but fortunately, there under the left wing was a grass covered aerodrome a little distance away. I stretched the glide as far as I could and only just made it. In fact I landed just inside the boundary fence and pulled up before reaching the track which formed the circumference of the main field. Given the informality of my preparations for the flight I couldn't have picked a worse place to land. It was Upavon, the headquarters of the training command. First on the scene was the Station Warrant Officer, who took me to the Chief Flying Instructor and the Chief Ground instructor. With no flight plan, I had in their eyes broken every rule in the book. Before I was allowed to proceed I had to produce a plan which passed their careful scrutiny. I was made very humble. However once away I had a good look at Stonehenge, and followed the railway line back to Exeter".

Jim's death also had a devastating effect on his girlfriend who lived in Auckland. Peter visited her after he returned from England but as so often happened, the family lost touch."

Sergeant James Harold Barry
Navigator
Sergeant William Howard Warren

11th November 1942

Lancaster W4262 of 57 Squadron was one of 42 aircraft dispatched to lay mines in the Gironde Estuary near Bordeaux, whilst others in the same force were sent to the Frisian Islands. All aircraft returned safely from the target area, but W4262 was one of two aircraft lost over English soil, both due to bad visibility. The weather at Scampton was sufficiently bad for a diversion to Tangmere to be ordered.

However, the 2000 foot cloud base, 2-3 miles visibility and only slight precipitation may have persuaded Flight Sergeant Abercrombie that a landing at base was still feasible. Everything appeared to be going well and the crew of W4262 were in frequent contact with the Air Traffic Control tower at Scampton.

At twenty five minutes past midnight, they acknowledged a magnetic bearing given to them from base. These were to be the last words anyone would hear from the crew.

An 83 Squadron Lancaster aircraft

Flight Sergeant Abercrombie and his crew had taken off from Scampton at 5:21pm on 10th November 1942, but the 11th was just 30 minutes old when they crashed only 400 ft above mean sea-level at Burgh on Bain near Binbrook in the Lincolnshire Wolds. There appears to be some confusion as to the exact date of death as some of the gravestones show the 10th. However, the accident report is clear that the aircraft crashed on the 11th.

Sgt J H Barry

Sergeant Warren was a member of the Royal Australian Air Force and was from Punchbowl, New South Wales originally enlisting in the Air force in Sydney. Sergeant Barry was a member of the Royal New Zealand Air Force and was from Rumuera, Auckland.

Also killed were, Flight Sergeant Ronald Ross Abercrombie (Pilot). He was the son of Doctor and Mrs R H Abercrombie and the husband of Wilma Young Abercrombie of Glasgow. He is commemorated in Glasgow Crematorium. Sergeant Andrew Bradshaw Jackson (Flight Engineer) who is buried in Macclesfield Cemetery. Flight Sergeant Michael Gerrard Everard (Wireless Operator) who is buried in Navan Cemetery, Ireland. Sergeant John Ernest Young (Air Gunner) who is buried in Wallasey Cemetery and Sergeant Frederick Oswald Button (Air Gunner), who is buried in Thurrock Cemetery.

The arrival of the heavy four engine bombers such as the Lancaster, Halifax and Stirling in late 1942 allowed for heavier bomb loads to be transported longer distances thus aiding the war effort. But, as this crash shows there was a major downside, such aircraft carried a crew of seven or eight and consequently more lives were at risk with each crash.

An 83 Squadron Lancaster landing on Runway 01 at Scampton in 1942

Sergeant Keith Paterson Mercer
Pilot
Sergeant Albert Edward Trott
Air Gunner
Flying Officer Frank Mayes
Bomb Aimer / Navigator
Flight Sergeant Archie Edward Shelson
Wireless Operator / Air Gunner

13th November 1942

King George VI meets aircrews of 57 Squadron 1942

For the previous two days, the whole of 5 Group were stood down whilst King George VI visited Scampton to present awards and decorations to the personnel there. However, by the 13th November 1942 it was back to work as normal.

Sergeant Mercer, the pilot of Lancaster R5569, was new to the aircraft having only twenty hours on type, eight of which were at night. Like all new crews, before they could fly the Lancaster operationally they were required to fly a number of "Bullseye" training exercises. A "Bullseye" exercise was a mock bombing raid on a distant town in the UK. The exercise tested night navigation skills and the teamwork of the newly formed crews.

Obviously no bombs were carried, but searchlight crews would try to find them in as realistic a way as they could without the anti-aircraft guns firing on them.

On 13th November Mercer and his crew were tasked to carry out a "Bullseye" mission. Having completed their exercise just before 11pm, Mercer and the rest of his 97 Squadron crew were returning to Scampton to land.

Having misjudged his approach the pilot elected, correctly, to apply power and go around for another attempt. However, inexperience took its toll once again. He raised the flaps too early and compounded the problem by entering a right hand turn.

As a result the aircraft stalled and crashed at 10:50pm at Brattleby, close to the airfield boundary. Six of the seven crew on board died instantly, four lie buried at Scampton. Sergeant Kenneth Collings was the only one to survive the initial impact, but he too died the next day in the military hospital at Bracebridge Heath and is buried in Southampton Cemetery. Sergeant Cyril Plimmer was interred in Enfield Crematorium and Flying Officer Jack Marshall was buried in Plumstead Cemetery, London.

Sergeant Mercer was a Canadian from Montreal with an obvious passion for aviation. As well as undertaking a correspondence course in aeronautical engineering, he had joined the RCAF straight from School in 1938 and served for two years as an Aircraftman on 115 Squadron. On leaving for civilian employment he became an Aircraft Apprentice. His hobbies were model building, photography and playing the piano.

He re-enlisted to the air force on the 20th May 1941 in Montreal. Having arrived at Scampton on 23rd October 1942, he had been on 97 Squadron less than a month when he was killed.

Archie Shelson was from Beausejour, Manitoba in Canada. He too had been on the Squadron less than a month when he was killed. Leaving school in 1939 he had worked as a Store Clerk, before joining the air force a year later. Describing himself as mechanically inclined he also enjoyed playing baseball and football.

Flight Sergeant Thomas Norman MacLeod
Air Gunner

10th December 1942

On 9th December 1942, two hundred and twenty seven aircraft took off to attack Turin in Italy. This was a long mission and involved a hazardous transit over the Alps. Turin had been bombed heavily the night before and was to receive a third raid the following night.

The first raid had devastated the city, but ironically the smoke, still rising from its smouldering buildings, helped to obscure it from this latest wave of bombers. As part of the mission, Avro Lancaster W4250 had taken off from Scampton at 5:46pm with Canadian Warrant Officer Gordon Ramey at the controls.

Approximately nine hours later, in the early hours of the morning of 10th December, a witness at Coningsby airfield saw the aircraft, presumably on approach into Woodhall Spa. He stated that the engines on the aircraft seemed to fail and shortly thereafter the aircraft stalled and crashed.

It was thought at the time that the engines might have failed due to mishandling of the aircraft's fuel system. Of the crew of eight, there were initially three survivors from the crash, but two of them, both air gunners, Flight Sergeant Macleod and Sergeant James Forbes Macpherson died later in the RAF Hospital at Rauceby. Twenty-six year old Macleod died on 2th December and twenty two year old Macpherson on the 13th. The only survivor, Sergeant W. O. Lundy appears to have made it through the war.

Crash investigators found a portion of the flight engineer's log in the wreckage. This showed that an engine had failed over the target and the crew had shut it down when they saw steam emanating from it. On only 3 engines, the Lancaster would have had to climb back over the Alps and faced a long transit to base at a much slower speed.

It would seem that, having used more fuel than expected, the crew forgot to change from the port centre tank, to the port inner. It was found later that the port centre was empty, but the port inner contained 60 Gallons. Due to the fact that the aircraft was in a left hand turn just before the crash, the last dregs of fuel would have moved to one side of the tank, causing all 3 remaining engines to fail at the same time from fuel starvation.

By now, the aircraft was far too low to change tanks and restart the engines, none the less the pilot attempted this and at the last moment changed tanks. However, his valiant efforts to save his stricken aircraft went un rewarded.

Sergeant Macpherson is buried in Windsor Cemetery. Warrant Officer Ramey is buried in Coningsby Cemetery, which is adjacent to the airfield, alongside fellow Canadian crew members, twenty two year old Flight Sergeant Raymond Dion and Pilot Officer Joseph McLaughlin. The other crew member killed that night was thirty year old Sergeant Kenneth William Pharoah who is buried in Marley Hill Churchyard, Newcastle.

Thomas Macleod was from Innisfail, Alberta, Canada. His service record shows that his last home leave was between the 2nd and 16th February 1942. This would have been the last time his parents Norman and Jennie Macleod would have seen him.

Ground crew work on a 57 Squadron Lancaster at Scampton

In civilian life he had been a hardware clerk. After the crash he was initially admitted to Station Sick Quarters at Scampton. He was diagnosed with a dislocated right elbow, a lacerated right knee and shock. However, his injuries must have been more serious or else complications developed because he was dead within 48 hours.

Flight Sergeant Elliot Livesey Cole
Pilot
Flying Officer Frank Ridley
Navigator
Flight Sergeant Llewellyn Grey
Bomb Aimer
Sergeant James Arthur Gerald Browne
Wireless Operator / Air Gunner
Sergeant Frederick Stanley Tristram Pittard
Flight Engineer

31st January 1943

1943 had arrived and by this time in the war, technology was being developed that improved bombing accuracy. One of these was H2S radar, this was the targeting device that Bomber Command had needed so badly. The ground mapping radar could give the Navigator an image of the target city at night and even through dense cloud. The radar was so advanced that there were serious concerns as to whether it should be used over enemy territory.

A shot down aircraft equipped with H2S would hand the Germans a weapon that could be used to equally devastating effect on British cities. However, the advantages were simply too great to ignore and on the 30th of January 1943 twelve Halifax and twelve Stirling bombers of the Pathfinder force employed their new H2S radar sets to mark the city of Hamburg with Target Indicator Flares.

The following force of 148 aircraft, mostly Lancasters, would attack with a combination of high explosive bombs and incendiaries.

On this first raid using H2S, the results can only be described as moderately successful, starting 119 fires in the city. As the crews became more familiar with H2S and the equipment received upgrades, bombing results became much more accurate. In fact, when the head of the Luftwaffe, Herman Goering was given a demonstration of a later captured H2S set he exclaimed "My God the British really can see in the dark".

One of the 148 Lancaster bombers on the raid was ED428 flown by Flight

Sergeant Cole, a 23 year old from Caulfield, Victoria, Australia with his crew of six. His was one of five Lancasters to be lost following this raid to Hamburg.

As eleven of the 49 squadron's aircraft returned to Fiskerton in the early hours of the following morning the weather that greeted them was atrocious. A 600 feet cloud base with 600 yards visibility in driving rain. The advice from the WAAF controller in the control tower was to divert to a base with better weather. This was advisory and the decision whether to divert or land was one which pilot of each aircraft would need to make for themselves.

Four of 49 squadron's aircraft took that advice, the remainder elected to land at Fiskerton. All except Flight Sergeant Cole's aircraft landed safely. There is some suggestion that his aircraft had been hit by flak and this may have influenced his decision to land as soon as possible at Fiskerton, it may also have made his aircraft more difficult to handle.

After locating the flare path, Cole made an approach from the North West onto one of Fiskerton's short runways. At 7:15am, Cole lost his battle to land his stricken aircraft when it collided with trees and crashed close to the Grimsby to Lincoln railway line. Six of the crew of seven were killed. Five of them are buried at Scampton. There was only one survivor, the Mid-upper Gunner Sergeant E Phillips, who escaped with unspecified injuries. The Rear Gunner, Sergeant William Wood was buried in Manor Park Cemetery, Essex.

Mrs Vi Hulbert, the wife of the Padre who was later to bury the crew, recalls the Christmas she had just shared with them: "One Christmas I played the American organ in the large hangar on the aerodrome at Fiskerton It was Christmas morning; what a wonderful service we had and a grand turnout of airmen and WAAF. My husband conducted the service. It was a bitterly cold morning, with a strong wind blowing, but the singing of the Christmas hymns and carols by this large congregation was something to remember. We managed to have services on all the five bomber stations that morning and afterwards my husband and I were invited to lunch at one of the stations.

In the evening we returned to Scampton where they were having a dance. I noticed Llewellyn, who was an Australian aircrew officer looking so sad and not joining in. My husband and I asked if he and his friend Jerry would like to go with us to another station which we had to visit and then they could come back to our billet with us.

Llewellyn was very upset because he had not heard from his people in Australia for Christmas, the mails were late. Jerry, his Australian friend, had just been married and he did not get Christmas leave. I think we were able to help them that night, though we did not get back to our billet until very late, but they enjoyed talking to us.

I told them that if they would like to come to us for Christmas Dinner my husband and I would be delighted, as we were hoping to have Boxing Night for our Christmas. They were delighted to come. I managed to buy a chicken at the NAAFI store and a plum pudding. It was very difficult for me to get food as I only had my civilian ration book.

They were so pleased as I had some tinned grapefruit, which I had brought, from our Rectory store cupboard when we left. It was Australian grapefruit, and this seemed to delight them. We had such a happy evening and it seemed to cheer them up.

Donald, my husband, drove them back to Scampton. The following week I remember so well, a cold snowy morning with a very strong wind blowing. Donald had gone to Scampton to welcome the aircrews back from operations. I was dressing and standing by my dressing table when I heard the roar of a plane, which seemed terribly low and somehow I sensed that it was in difficulty.

I knew that Llewellyn and Jerry had gone on operations the night before and I felt so anxious somehow, as if I almost knew that it was going to be bad news. Donald came back to our billet and I knew directly he came into our room by the expression on his face, that all was not well. I asked him if all the planes had landed safely on the aerodrome. He replied, 'I'm afraid not.' I asked, 'Was it Llewellyn and Jerry and their crew?' Donald replied, 'Yes.' It did not seem possible somehow that they had returned safely from operations only to crash and all be killed. It was their plane that I had heard flying so low and circling round trying to land.

It was another of the many funerals that were held in the village church at Scampton, followed by full RAF burial ceremony, which I had to attend. Donald conducted the service - Jerry's wife and many relatives were there. After the service I went to speak to Jerry's wife and the first thing she said was 'Thank you for having Jerry out at Christmas. He wrote and told me all about it'. What a wonderful spirit of selflessness she showed, and how brave, not thinking of her own sorrow, remembering to say thank you to me".

Sgt Grey's original grave marker cross

Reverend Hulbert officiates at the funeral of Flight Sergeant Cole's crew

Flying Officer John Fergus Greenan
Pilot
Sergeant Harold William Ricketts
Wireless Operator / Air Gunner
Sergeant John Burns Mallett
Flight Engineer
Flight Sergeant Frederick Warren Music
Navigator
Sergeant Frank Cyril Edward Miller
Air Gunner

2nd March 1943

To the aircrews of Bomber Commander Berlin was known as the Big City. At the mid-afternoon briefing on the upper floor of the Airmen's Mess, when the curtain over the map of Europe was drawn back by the briefing officer to reveal Berlin as the target, an audible sigh would be heard throughout the room.

Once again they would be facing Germany's most formidable defences. This was not just a very long mission; this one would be to the most heavily defended city in the world. Night fighters would dog them all the way to the target, but even they wouldn't follow the bombers over Berlin and with good reason, the Flak was ferocious and indiscriminate. Still far from home, the returning bombers would trek westward over Europe, facing yet more night fighters.

The raid itself was considered to be highly successful, and the post attack report leaves no doubt how happy 57 Squadron were with the results: "Six aircraft are known to have reached the target area where visibility was good above haze. The Path Finder Force markers were seen in the city area and many crews saw their bombs fall in the built-up part of the town. Huge fires resulted which could be seen for nearly 200 miles on the return journey. A very successful raid."

At 2am on the 2nd March 1943, the crew of Lancaster R5894 must have considered themselves very lucky, for they had survived the ordeal of a long mission across Nazi occupied Europe. Just moments from touch-down at Scampton, disaster struck. All that is known for certain is that just before the crash, the aircraft's port wing struck High Tension cables at Riseholme, three miles south of the airfield.

Although the reason for the crash has always remained a mystery, there was a great deal of speculation that they had collided with Waddington based Lancaster ED490, belonging to 9 Squadron. This aircraft crashed at around the same time, just a few miles away at Heighington.

In his report on the accident, the Officer Commanding 57 Squadron had the following to say:

> *"The aircraft was returning from an operational sortie and crashed short of the aerodrome. I consider something unusual must have occurred, such as a collision or being badly damaged by an enemy night fighter, or flak as Flying Officer Greenan was a reliable and good pilot."*

The Station Commander, Group Captain Whitworth agreed with this and like others on the station he must have known that this tragedy came when 57 Squadron were under particular pressure to produce results. The 57 Squadron F540 (Squadron Log) for March 1943, illustrates just what pressures they were under and how well they coped:

> *"During March 1943, No. 57 Squadron operated on sixteen occasions, detailing 127 sorties, of which 102 were completed, and involving 740.40 hours of flying. This was a considerable increase on last month and was the heaviest month's work since the Squadron converted to Lancaster aircraft. This fine effort was achieved with an effective strength of two flights, because although a third flight was started on the 16th March two circumstances counterbalanced that - vis, on the morning of 15th March, nine aircraft were destroyed or seriously damaged by a series of accidental explosions which occurred amongst bombed up aircraft parked on the perimeter track, following the cancellation at a late hour of operations ordered the previous day; and secondly, five experienced crews were posted on March 26th to the newly formed No. 617 Squadron."*

These were tumultuous times at Scampton and only Wing Commander Guy Gibson and a few other senior officers at Scampton knew that in less than two months Scampton's fame would be secured with the legendary Dambusters raid of 617 Squadron. The total security around this mission goes some way to explaining the note of resentment 57 Squadron's F540 (Daily Log) writer seems to give at the loss of five experienced crews.

John Greenan was from Calgary, Alberta where he worked for the Royal Bank of Canada. He had joined the bank in 1937 as a junior clerk and by the time he left in 1940 had worked his way up to ledger keeper. His hobbies were typically Canadian and he enjoyed Hockey, Baseball, Curling, Tennis and Golf. He qualified as a pilot on 20th September 1941, but had only been with 57 Squadron for three months at the time of the crash.

John Greenan

John Mallett was from Palmerston, Ontario where he had worked as a Farmer and Beekeeper. His interviewing officer assessed him as having a keen intellect with a neat, clean-cut and athletic appearance. He enjoyed hockey, softball, swimming and soccer. He too had been with 57 Squadron for just three months.

Above: Wing Commander Guy Gibson (front right) with other aircrew and his dog "Nigger"
Below: Lancaster of 617 Squadron modified to carry Dr Barnes Wallis's specially designed dam busting weapon (original photograph - quality as good as it came)

Life on 57 Squadron
by Flight Lieutenant Stevie Stevens DFC AE

I joined 57 Squadron at Scampton, north of Lincoln, on 1st May 1943 and soon acquired Lancaster ED946 "E" as my brand new personal aircraft. After carrying out several tests for performance, speed, fuel consumption weaponry and instrument calibration we spent some time on practice bombing and gunnery. We were ready for war!

My only trip as second pilot was to Duisberg on 12th May with Sqn Ldr Smith. He also took my Flight Engineer and my Bomb Aimer. Long before we arrived at the target the Ruhr flak batteries put up a huge barrage. 88mm heavy batteries blasted the air with heavy explosions which rocked the aircraft while lighter flak streamed up like flaming onions. The whole scene was lit up by searchlights which turned night into day. On our return, we found that 34 of our aircraft had been shot down including from our squadron. Several other aircraft were badly damaged. With another 29 trips ahead, I thought my survival chances were small.

From the 13th - 23rd. of May I flew by day and night continuing to gain experience by practice bombing, gunnery, navigation and instrument flying. The magnetic compass was "swung", the bombsight levelled and the gun turrets tested. The front gun turret had a faulty rotating servo joint, which would spray the windscreen with a light oil, and on two occasions I had to land the aircraft at night peering through the small clear vision panel. This was a useful exercise as there were later occasions when the windscreen became so thickly coated with ice that forward vision was negligible.

On 16th. May I had to wait for a 617 flight to take off. We had noticed the modified bomb bays earlier. They looked like huge dustbins mounted laterally. Just after I landed a 617 aircraft followed. The pilot was very upset. He was flying so low over the sea his weapon had struck the water and broken away. Later on we heard some of the aircraft returning. 617 Squadron had become the "Dam Busters" and made their name in history.

Exactly one week later, on 23rd May. I flew my first trip as a Lancaster Captain to bomb Dortmund. As the bombs left the aircraft I felt a moment of exhilaration. Two years earlier the Germans had dropped a bomb on my house temporarily burying my parents and destroying all my belongings save for a school prize and a pair of Scout shorts. Now I thought I had paid the debt I owed. Although two fighters made a pass at us, we returned safely. Thirty eight aircraft were shot down including two from my Squadron. My crew and I enjoyed nine days leave. I wondered if we should survive to enjoy another.

Sergeant Jack Saul Lockwood
Pilot

13th August 1943

Jack Lockwood

This grave is unique at Scampton in that it is not associated with RAF Scampton, but rather the private burial of a local man serving at another unit. Jack Lockwood was the second pilot of a Wellington XII (MP630) of 172 Squadron Coastal Command. The aircraft had left RAF Chivenor in Devon on an anti-submarine patrol. Returning to base at 4:30 in the morning, in bad weather, the aircraft struck a building on a nearby ridge and was completely destroyed when the depth charges on board exploded. All six crew were killed instantly.

The grave is to the rear of the churchyard in a plot away from the majority of RAF burials. Jack's parents who both died in the early 1970's are buried next to him. He is also commemorated with a stone plaque on the wall just inside the Church door.

Jack had grown-up at Scampton Houses, just behind the church; he was a very keen horseman and had won many point-to-point events. Coming from a family with a strong farming tradition he had himself pursued a career as a farmer. In 1938 he had taken over the running of Spridlington Grange farm and was enjoying his new life as a farmer in his own right.

At the outbreak of war Jack was in a cinema in Lincoln when an army Major made an appeal for new recruits. As a horseman, the Leicestershire Yeomanry and its cavalry appealed to him and he volunteered at once. However, the regiment's move away from horses to tanks did not hold as much appeal and he applied to transfer to the Royal Air Force. Jack began his flying training in Canada and whilst there he met a girl called Elaine McInnes and the pair formed a close friendship. Years later Elaine, who was by now a nun, travelled to England to investigate Jack's crash and to visit the station where he was based.

Jack in war time flying kit

IN EVERLASTING REMEMBRANCE
JACK SAUL
ELDER SON OF
WILLIAM S & MARGARET E. LOCKWOOD
SGT/PILOT COASTAL COMMAND
KILLED ON OPERATIONS
AUG 1943
AGED YRS.

THEY DIED
THAT WE MIGHT LIVE IN FREEDOM

Pilot Officer Jack Smithers
Pilot
Flight Sergeant Ronald Henry Haskins
Air Gunner

16th August 1943

Lancaster JA896 of 57 Squadron was returning from an eight-hour bombing mission to Milan in Northern Italy. It had been Jack Smithers' first operational flight and tragically it would also turn out to be his last.

It was just after 4:30 in the morning and he and his crew were already in trouble. The port outer engine had failed and to reduce the drag created by a dead engine, the propeller blades were turned edge on to the airflow, in a process known as feathering. Later investigation would show that the engine had suffered some form of over-heating, although the exact nature of the problem was never determined.

A landing with a failed engine is difficult at the best of times, but after a harrowing eight-hour mission it could be so much more demanding for a tired pilot. On landing, the Lancaster hit the ground very heavily and bounced. Electing to go-around for another approach Jack was too hasty in applying the power.

Due to having only three engines there was much greater power on the starboard wing. The aircraft then began to veer to port, a well understood phenomenon, known to the pilots of the day as swing. The aircraft's port wing then struck the ground and spun the aircraft through 180 degrees. Such was the speed of the aircraft that it flipped inverted and caught fire, killing five of its crew and injuring two others in the process.

> The 57 Squadron accident report summed up as follows:
>
> *"The aircraft made a steady approach on these three engines well in line with the contact strip which was in use at the time. Aircraft bounced badly on touching down and an attempt was made to go around again by opening the three good engines to full power. The resulting swing from this procedure caught the pilot unawares and due to his inexperience resulted in his losing control of the aircraft. Concrete evidence is not possible due to the death of the pilot."*

Jack Smithers was a Flight Sergeant at the time of the accident, but unbeknown to him, he had already been selected for a commission on 13th July 1943 and was duly buried as a Pilot Officer. He was married to Nancy Rose Smithers and lived in Armidale, New South Wales where he had worked as an assistant in the Postmaster General's Department. He was only 22 when he died.

Hospital at Rauceby. However, his injuries were too severe and he died less than four hours later. He was originally from Inglewood in Western Australia and was single.

Also killed were Pilot Officer Arthur Joseph Organ who was buried in Bristol, Sergeant Derrick John Rose, buried in London and Sergeant Alan George Luxford, buried in Sheffield. Pilot Officer Bladen and Sergeant Burgess both survived with minor injuries and seem to have gone on to survive the war.

Sergeant Frederick Douglas Grant
Wireless Operator / Air Gunner

10th November 1943

At seven minutes to seven on 10th November 1943, Lancaster ED812 took-off from RAF Swinderby on a Bullseye training mission. The majority of the mission seems to have gone well, but at 9:45pm the aircraft dived at great speed and smashed into fields near Dunholme Lodge.

The speed of the Lancaster's terminal dive was so great that the outer portions of each wing could not stand the strain and broke off. Post crash investigation revealed that the aircraft had suffered an in flight fire, but could not determine whether this had been the reason that control of the aircraft was lost or not.

Air crews would have little chance of escape from an ensuing fire even if they survived the crash

The Flying Control Officer at RAF Dunholme Lodge witnessed the crash. Upon hearing a loud explosion, he rushed outside onto the balcony of the control tower. Once outside, he saw an aircraft emerge from the clouds burning fiercely. The aircraft, which had already lost its tail, crashed on the rear of the Officers' Mess. The entire crew was killed instantly, however there were no casualties on the ground.

Also killed and buried where indicated were Pilot Officer Sydney George Scutt who is buried in Fulham, Sergeant Clifford Walter Henry Baughen in Lambeth, Sergeant Ian Clark Brough in Perth, Flying Officer John Kidston Law Paterson in Knutsford, Sergeant William Halliwell in Manchester, Aircraftman First Class Neville Wade, in Woking and Sergeant Eric William Plowman in Yeovil Cemetery.

The Western Gazette of 19 November 1943 gives an interesting insight into the life of Sergeant Eric Plowman and how a private ceremony for those returned home for burial was often conducted:

"Mr. and Mrs. H.W. Plowman of Kasouli, 148 Ilchester Road, have received official notification that their only son, Sergeant Gunner Eric William Plowman, RAF, aged 19, has been killed on active service. Formerly a member of 1032 (Yeovil) Squadron, Air Training Corps, he joined the RAF eleven months ago and at the time of his death had almost completed his training. Educated at Yeovil School, he was employed at the office of Messrs. W.E. Plowman & Son Ltd., Vicarage Street for fourteen months, was a choirboy at St. Andrew's Church, Preston Grove and a member of the Crusaders. The interment at the Cemetery on Tuesday was preceded by a short service conducted by the Vicar of Yeovil (Rev. H. Mortlock Treen) and Rev. K. Puddy (curate). Three wreaths from service colleagues were placed on the coffin which was covered with the Union Jack. At the graveside ATC buglers sounded "Last Post" and "Reveille."

Corporal Arthur Edward Flello

21st August 1944

Arthur Flello was a Motor Transport driver based at Scampton, which by this time had become known as Number 52 Base. Originally from Offerton in Cheshire, he was married to Emily Elizabeth Flello. He was killed in a road traffic accident at Duddington near Stamford on 21st August 1944.

Feldwebel Heinrich Conze
Unteroffizier Rudolf Scherer
Unteroffizier Alfred Altenkirch
Obergerfreiter Wener Nollau

4th March 1945

Heinrich Conze

On this night, the Luftwaffe launched one of its deadliest attacks against Bomber Command. Operation Gisela was the German codename for what was to become their last attack on British soil.

The basic concept of the mission was that over 200 night fighters would merge with the returning bombers. Rather than attacking immediately, they would wait until the bombers were almost home. As the bombers prepared to land, they would turn on their landing lights and their gunners would not be expecting an attack.

Once the attack began, confusion would run wild amongst the bombers, making them easy targets. In the event, 24 RAF Bombers were shot down within site of home base that night and another 20 damaged.

This particular German crew began at around 0130 by attacking Lancaster NG502 of 460 Squadron, RAF Binbrook. The Lancaster crashed near Langworth killing two of its crew; Sergeant A Streatfield and Flight Sergeant R E Davey, both of whom are buried in Cambridge City Cemetery. Eye witnesses saw the German aircraft firing on the Lancaster and then flying off at low-level towards Scothern.

At the same time, Observer Jack Kelway who had joined the Royal Observer Corps on June 10th 1944 was driving towards his place of duty at the Love One Post in Hackthorn.

He had just left Welton heading North on the Spridlington road when his car was attacked from his right by cannon fire from the JU88 G6. However, the pilot misjudged his attack and crashed into the car. The impact hurled the car across two fields destroying it and the aircraft in the process, the four air crew and Kelway being killed instantly. This became the penultimate German aircraft to be lost over British soil. Indeed, the last one was lost only minutes later in almost identical circumstances.

At RAF Elvington near York, a Ju88 on the same mission had successfully attacked a Halifax and strafed a nearby airfield. It then opened fire on a passing taxi, which was travelling on a road close to the airfield. Again, the pilot flew too low and hit a farmhouse killing three civilians.

At this late stage of the war, blackout restrictions had been relaxed and car headlights may have been brighter than the enemy pilots were used to. This could have led them to believe they were aircraft landing lights.

It would seem possible that in the dark, both pilots mistook the car lights for an aircraft landing at the airfield. The fact that car lights are much closer together than a bombers might lead the pilot to believe that he was higher than in fact he was. This could explain why they flew such a dangerous mission only to attack two targets of no real military value.

Observer Jack Kelway

A monument in the front garden of the Farmhouse in memory of those killed

The farmhouse near York into which the German aircraft crashed

Jack Kelway was a well-known and popular figure in Lincoln. He was a Shift Superintendent at a local Sugar Beet factory and had served as a Special Constable for many years.

In the Royal Observer Corps, he was a particularly conscientious and enthusiastic member. When going on duty at Hackthorn, his usual practice was to drive there early and sleep at the post prior to his shift. On the night of his death he had broken from this routine and planned to arrive and go straight on duty, this in turn caused him to be in the wrong place at very much the wrong time.

In addition to his ROC duties, he also devoted time to teaching aircraft recognition at the local Air Training Corps Squadron at North Hykeham. His devotion to his duties was reflected in the number of local dignitaries that attended his funeral on the 7th of March. Inspector J C Ilman represented A Division of the Lincoln Special Constabulary, Observer Commander R R Poole the ROC, Mr J H Cargill represented his employers and the Lady Mayoress attended on behalf of the Mayor. Many of his colleagues at the Sugar Beet factory were also present; four of them were the coffin bearers. After the burial in Newport Cemetery, Lincoln, members of the Royal Observer Corps and Air Training Corps filed in pairs to the graveside and saluted their dead comrade.

Observer Kelway holds the dubious distinction of being the only member of the Royal Observer Corps killed on active duty whilst on home soil. All four Germans were buried at Scampton with full military honours the next day.

Kelway's somewhat unkempt grave (Foreground) not many metres from the immaculately maintained Commonwealth War Graves plot (Background) at Newport Cemetery in Lincoln

Flight Lieutenant Herbert Richard Birch
Pilot

22nd January 1951

Herbert Birch was the pilot of De Havilland Mosquito TA701 of 139 Sqn based at RAF Hemswell. On the night of 22nd January 1951, he and his navigator Flight Lieutenant G T Burnie had been detailed to conduct shallow dive bombing attacks on the practice range at Wainfleet, just to the south of Skegness.

At night, it is often possible for the pilot to fly visually once they have climbed to sufficient altitude and the horizon can be distinguished with the aid of starlight. However, as they descend, the horizon once again becomes indistinct and it is important that the pilot makes the transition back to instrument flying.

On this occasion, Herbert Birch left that transition just a few seconds too late and in doing so delayed his pull out of the dive. The Mosquito hit the ground at a shallow angle and crashed. Flight Lieutenant Birch was killed, but his navigator Flight Lieutenant Burnie survived.

Like so many aviation disasters, there was an extremely narrow margin between a routine flight and catastrophe. Just a few feet higher and both would have returned to Hemswell, probably without even realising how close they had come to the ground.

Flight Lieutenant Graham Wilfred Peter
Pilot
Sergeant Kenneth Ireson
Navigator
Sergeant Patrick Edward Clark
Air Gunner
Sergeant Arthur John Fitzgerald
Air Gunner

14th July 1951

It was the 14th July 1951 and the weather at Scampton was less than ideal for night flying training. The cloud-base was down to 200ft and visibility below that was only 3000yds. The pilot of Avro Lincoln RA692, Graham Peter was attached to 230 Operational Conversion Unit (OCU) and was learning to fly the RAF's most capable strategic bomber of the time.

A Lincoln Bomber displayed at the Cosford Air Museum

The aircraft had been designed in World War Two as a development of the famous Lancaster, but the changes made were so radical that it had to be regarded as a totally new aircraft type and it became known as the Lincoln.

Training new pilots is always a balance of ensuring that they have the necessary skills and letting them fly solo to develop those skills.

In this case, it looks likely that an error of judgment had been made and with only seven hours of night flying experience, Flight Lieutenant Peter had been put in command of a four-engine heavy bomber and its crew of six to practice night landings.

Due to the poor weather, Flight Lieutenant Peter was making a Beam Approach to Scampton. At some point, he must have decided that his aircraft had drifted off the approach and that he should go-around for another try.

This is where inexperience took its toll, attempting to climb away with full landing flap still selected, the pilot lost control and at 03:12 in the morning the aircraft crashed at Welton Grange Farm. Missing the farmhouse by just 300 yards, the occupants were quickly awoken by the explosion. First on the scene was the Dairyman Norman Crowson, but the fierce flames of the kerosene-fuelled fire prevented any attempt at rescue.

It was later found that the entire crew had in any case been killed instantly on impact. Mrs Mary Wade, who also lived at the farm, gave her account to the Lincolnshire Echo of what must clearly have been a terrifying sight as follows.

> *"I was awakened by a terrific roar as the plane went over. It took off some tiles and then I saw something like a flash of lightning. There was a terrific explosion that shook the building. I went to my bedroom and saw that the plane was a mass of flames"*

The aircraft had crashed into a field occupied by 50 pedigree Ayrshire cattle. Despite the wreckage being spread over a wide area, the cattle had a remarkably lucky escape as they were all completely uninjured.

As well as those buried at Scampton, Flying Officer F Cousins DFC and Bar of Wakefield, Sergeant E Newman of Middlesbrough, Sergeant A J Fitzgerald of Ontario Canada and Cadet Engineer N Moss of Ealing were also killed. The investigation into the accident revealed the inadequate night flying training that Flight Lieutenant Peter had received and made the following recommendation:

> *"Pilots selected for courses at No 230 OCU should have at least 10 hours recent solo experience at night as captain on Wellington or comparable aircraft"*

The following gives a remarkable insight into the shock of receiving the news of the loss of a loved one, particularly at a time of peace, coming, as it did, six years after the end of the Second World War. Alice Patricia Clark writes about the death of Sergeant Patrick Edward Clark in this incident:

A Knock At The Door by Alice Patricia (Pat) Clark (nee Paterson)

When the telegram arrived I was bathing Eileen; still not much more than a baby, not quite 15 months old and minus her twin, little Michael, dead at 6 months of age. My husband . . . . . KILLED?

The RAF was a kind of euphemism for a shadowy hinterland inhabited by Eddie and his colleagues, but not one that I had visualized death in! The death of my young man; my child's father - father-to-be of my unborn child. So young to die - with not even the hostilities of war as any sort of reason for his death.

I had looked upon the Forces as being a world in which protection was taken for granted; security a right, that could guarantee, or indeed protection was taken for granted; security a right, that could guarantee, or indeed should guarantee, liberty and safety

As I tried desperately to digest and accept what I was reading, I had the overwhelming feeling of a great need to be alone; a feeling I could not indulge in. I had my baby daughter to consider. Grief was a liberty I simply could not afford for her sake and the sake of the child growing inside me, who both needed the calm of a concerned mother; not the utter panic that was at that moment coursing through my mind and body.

As I was vainly attempting to digest the first telegram, hoping that somehow it was a horrible dream, or a bad joke, a knock at the door heralded the certainty of yet another nightmarish piece of news.

For a few seconds I allowed myself to hope "maybe it's Eddie?" He's home to tell us it's all a gross mistake. I almost ran to answer the knock, so vivid was my hope. I pulled the door open with great face, actually anticipating his "Hello"; his reassurance. His very presence had become such a vivid hope . . . . But it was not to be. . . . ."Mrs Clark?" It was a second telegram giving more details of the tragedy that had taken Eddie's life at 26 years old!

After these two telegrams, the second being pages long; for me it seemed to be a whole lot of nothing; a vacuum, that was creating a macabre state of oblivion compounding my reaction to this news, which was slowly, but surely mounting to manic proportions. But, the outside world was normal; the sun shone; the traffic noise was still there. The sounds of people - still there, still passing by - How can everything remain normal when my life has just been shattered beyond belief? Yet my mind was racing. I found myself thinking of and remembering in detail the only time in my life I had had too much to drink!

I was remembering because it was also the night Eddie and I first met. Back then I was attempting to appear normal in speech and actions just as I must also do now. But in the humour of my actions that day there was no similarity to the terror of trying to do the same now, on this day of horrifying news. Now all of my actions were becoming complex rituals; each of my steps seemed to be leading nowhere. Total disorientation overtook my very being - yet I found some sort of strength to think I must not let anyone know of my terror, nor must anyone think I won't get through the panic.

For my children's sake I must get through it. It will be a lesson I'll teach myself in surviving - but - how long will it take? Will it be one year?. . . twenty years? The answer is . . . I was 21 years old when I received those telegrams but I never have gotten over it, even all these years later my mind and thoughts can transfer so easily and with acute clarity, back to that day that changed my life forever.

In one moment of time I was transformed from being married, mother of twins, one dead, pregnant again and husband killed. I was a widow and not yet 22 years old.

My greatest source of joy, my children, especially Ken - he has grown to manhood now and is so very much like Eddie that my carefully built up guard occasionally slips and a few tears trickle down my cheeks as I look at Ken . . . . and see only his dad, Eddie!! Eddie always said if it's a boy we'd call him Kenneth after his navigator. "A boy should know where he's going in life and how to get there."

Unexpected knocks at my door, all these years later, still hold fear and panic for me in a pavlovian reflex . . . . I still feel my heart thud with trepidation as I go to do what should be a basic and simple task - to answer the knock at the door.

Eddie, home on leave in the late 1940s

Treasured Clark family photographs showing the funeral and the full Military Honours accorded it.

In the bottom picture, Mrs Clark is the lady in the light coloured beret behind the stooping RAF Sergeant. At the time she was 5 months pregnant with son Ken

Sergeant Edgar John Smith
Air Gunner

1st December 1951

The Korean War was at its height. After very nearly being driven from the Korean Peninsula, Allied forces had fought back but had reached a stalemate at the 38th parallel. The war would go on for more than a year with the ever-present threat of another push by the Chinese using their human wave theory of warfare. The tactic was simple, overwhelm your enemy with shear weight of numbers and defeat their technological advantage.

It was now clear to the British Government that the post World War 2 peace dividend was over. Conscription was reintroduced and a massive programme of re-armament was developed. Those training new pilots and crews for the Avro Lincoln on 230 Operational Conversion Unit would no doubt have been under considerable pressure to provide more crews for duty on the frontline.

Although RAF Lincolns did not fight in Korea, they were still at the forefront in the fight against communism. Flying against the Mau Mau in Kenya and for a while carrying the British nuclear deterrent.

The pilot of Lincoln B2 RF567 was Sergeant George Watson from Harrogate. Although he had been flying for two and a half years years, his first flight in a Lincoln had only taken place a day before the accident. On the day of the accident, he had flown with his instructor, Flight Lieutenant Clarringbull, who later stated that he had done very well and seemed fully competent to fly solo.

At 11:40am Watson and his crew took-off on a solo flight for the first time. Very quickly things started to go wrong when the Flight Engineer reported that the number one engine oil temperature was too high. Watson ordered the engine to be shut down and the propeller feathered. Being so inexperienced on the Lincoln, it's hardly surprising that Watson misjudged his approach and landed just short of the runway.

The aircraft initially bounced but quickly veered off the runway centre line and headed towards Number 1 Hangar. At this time, Watson's instructor Flight Lieutenant Clarringbull came out of his office. He was later to give the following statement to the Coroner:

> *"I came out of my office and saw a Lincoln aircraft coming across the runway. Its Number one engine was feathered and the aircraft was very low. I saw it actually touchdown on the grass diagonally to the runway almost facing Number 1 hanger before it crashed"*

The inquest was in fact held in Station Sick Quarters at Scampton, whilst the three survivors of the crash were still patients there. Due to the fact that the pilot was amongst those who survived the crash, the inquest was able to establish all the factors that lead to the crash. In his summing up, the coroner, Mr H J J Griffith said:

> *"This is part of the price to be paid. You all know that rearmament has to be carried through and with a constantly expanding Air Force, accidents are bound to happen. These men died in the service of their country, just as much as if they were on active service"*

The crash claimed the lives of two Air Gunners airborne on this mission. Sergeant Smith who is buried at Scampton and Sergeant Gerald Leslie Laver of Wimbledon. The coroner noted that both had either died instantly or were rendered unconscious by the crash and he recorded a verdict of accidental death. Sergeant Smith was originally from Ashley Down, Bristol and was only 19 when he died.

An eye witness account by Peter Richmond

Peter with his friends Edward and Michael Hunn

Some experiences make such an impact on a young mind that they never seem to fade; what happened on Saturday 1st December 1951 is one such memory and, despite being almost fifty seven years ago, I still recall it clearly and certain smells bring it rushing to my mind.

It was an ordinary Saturday; I'd been to 'Saturday Cinema' at the Scampton picture house with two of my friends and returned home for lunch. My mother was busy and irritated that I hadn't picked up the spent fireworks in the garden despite it being three weeks since Bonfire Night and I was told: 'Do it or stay in all day!' So, rather than face a day of boredom I went into the garden

As I was collecting the by then soggy remains there was a loud noise accompanied by a rush of hot air which made me leap to my feet and look to the direction of the noise. What I saw froze me to the spot. Across the grass plot, beyond our married quarter garden, and almost directly in front of me, were the tangled remains of a Lincoln Bomber. The aircraft was laying nose towards me at an angle with flames and smoke bursting out of it.

The tail must have broken away as I could also see the rear turret. My brain seemed to be taking the sight in at speeds which put everything into slow motion and only the sight of a burning figure running from the front of the aircraft broke the shock which rooted me to the ground.

I rushed into the kitchen to be met by my mother who seemed to think I had caused the noise by knocking over a bag of coke in the shed and before I had a chance to speak, a quick clip round the ear was dispensed at the mere thought of the mess I might have created. My mouth was open but no words would come out, so I grabbed her by the arm and pulled her to the window jabbing my finger in the direction of the crash. All that was now visible of the aircraft was a deep orangey - red glow shrouded by dense black smoke.

Within seconds Mum had dragged me to the front door to escape the danger. Once outside we could hear the reports as the ammunition of the aircraft's guns were set off by the heat of the fire. The usually quiet street was filled by adults all trying to find out what had happened. A black pall of oily smoke began to drift over the street and the acrid stink made it impossible to stay. We, and the other residents, made our way to other houses which were not so badly affected.

The day continued in an atmosphere of great concern, not simply because of the tragedy, but also because my friend Michael was missing for some hours. It turned out that he had spent the day watching the Firemen put out the fire and hose down the surrounding buildings to stop the fire from spreading. His mother was furious with him whereas I, like most other little boys, felt piqued that I had not been with him.

My father had gone off to work that morning and didn't return home again until the following day because he, as the Warrant Officer i/c MT (Motor Transport), had spent the afternoon and night assisting with the clean up operation.

Flying Officer Patrick Esmond Reeve
Pilot

27th March 1953

By now, Scampton had entered the jet-age with the arrival of the English Electric Canberra. The aircraft was a massive leap forward, flying twice as fast as the Lincoln, which it replaced. With this increased performance came increased risk, especially since the capabilities and limitations of jet aircraft were not yet fully understood.

Canberra WH669 of 10 Squadron was being flown from Scampton by its pilot, Flying Officer Reeve and his two crew, Pilot Officer John Golden Woods (Navigator Plotter) and Pilot Officer Vivian Owen (Navigator Observer).

Canberra at low level over Scampton - obviously on a press day

The crew had been on a continuation training sortie which had taken off at 2pm. Fifty minutes later the Canberra made a successful let down from high altitude and overshot Scampton to practice another. It is presumed that the aircraft was then climbed to 30,000 feet to position for a let down to Scampton once more.

For reasons that the Board of Enquiry were never able to establish, Pilot Officer Reeve lost control of the aircraft and it entered a high speed dive.

Although he tried everything in his power to slow the aircraft down, including extending the air brakes and opening the bomb bay, he was unsuccessful and the aircraft struck the ground at Dilhorne near Cheadle, just eleven minutes after departing Scampton.

Farm workers at the scene saw the aircraft at high level suddenly stall and go into a steep dive from which it did not recover. The pilot jettisoned the canopy, but was unable to effect an escape before the aircraft crashed. Although there is little left today to show that such dramatic events took place, a close examination of the crash scene will still reveal some scattered wreckage.

Sergeant Thomas Lewis Kendrick

20th March 1956

Sergeant Kendrick was an RAF Policeman serving with 1 Personnel Holding Unit at RAF Innsworth who died of natural causes.

Flight Lieutenant Dennis George Blackwell
Navigator Plotter

3rd   July 1958

Most accidents are a combination of seemingly unrelated events which conspire to bring about disaster. Each of the factors in an accident may not in themselves cause significant danger. But, when they happen together, the unfortunate set of coincidences can quickly lead to loss of life. Such was the case for Dennis Blackwell.

On the 2nd of July 1958, the ground-crew manoeuvring Vulcan B1 XH497 out of the hangar could have had no idea how an apparently minor incident would bring about the death of Flight Lieutenant Blackwell.

617 Squadron had received the Vulcan into service less than two months previously. As with all new aircraft types, both air and ground crews were learning how to handle the aircraft. As mentioned above, on the day prior to the accident, ground crew were using a Matador aircraft tug to push XH497 out of the hangar. During a left hand turn, the nose wheel was pushed beyond its design limits and the pivot bracket was fractured.

It is assumed that this damage went unnoticed and when XH497 took-off on a routine training flight the next day, part of the nose wheel fell off. The pilot, Flight Lieutenant Graham Smeaton now faced a very unusual dilemma, was it safer for his crew to remain with the aircraft and risk the consequences of a high-speed crash landing or should they bail-out and use their parachutes. Wisely choosing to get advice from the ground, he contacted the Officer Commanding 617 Squadron, Wing Commander Douglas Bower. Bower advised him to continue circling Scampton whilst he himself sought further advice. After an hour, it was decided that the three-rear crew should bail out over Waddington, after which Smeaton and his co-pilot, Flying Officer Wood would attempt a crash landing a Scampton.

Dennis Blackwell and his colleagues abandoned the aircraft at 3000 ft over Waddington. It was later reported that they did so very calmly and with the utmost professionalism. Unfortunately, a small error in the way Blackwell's parachute was rigged prevented it from opening correctly. One of the cords connecting the main parachute to the auxiliary had become fouled on the emergency oxygen supply. Dennis Blackwell was killed instantly when he struck the ground.

Ironically, Flight Lieutenant Smeaton was able to bring the Vulcan in for a near normal landing. Enough of the nose undercarriage survived to keep the aircraft's nose off the ground, causing only minor damage. Repairs were started on the day of the incident and it was expected that they would take less than a month to complete.

The inquest was held at RAF Waddington and this was not without controversy. The Coroner, Mr Pattinson was less than pleased to hear that a parachute expert from Farnborough would not be attending the inquest, and he let his feelings on the matter be known, saying: "This inquiry is in danger of becoming farcical without this expert"

XH497 once it had returned to service.

On a more conciliatory note, Mr Pattinson also said: "Whatever the evidence that comes out, I don't want anyone to blame themselves. If they are to be blamed by authority, that is a different matter, but they must not blame themselves - I do not wish anybody, pilot, packers or manufacturers, those who jumped - to blame themselves in anyway"

Recording a verdict of death by misadventure, Mr Pattinson summed up by saying: "I am in rather a difficult position. Naturally I would like to have asked the expert from Farnborough a lot of questions"

He also had the following remarks about the crew of XH497: "They were a brave lot. It must have been agonising for them, but these chaps were perfectly calm, ordered and disciplined. I really do not think I can lay blame at anybody's door in this matter"

It does seem that the coroner was not aware of a number of very pertinent facts. The mishandling of the aircraft on the day previous and the incorrectly packed parachute did not feature in the inquest. In those days, the RAF would have no desire to air its dirty laundry in public and perhaps the non-appearance of the parachute expert was a deliberate move to make sure any failings were not exposed.

Today, the RAF has a very different approach to such matters. The more thoroughly an accident is investigated and the more widely the lessons learnt are published, the greater the chance that it won't be repeated.

Flight Lieutenant Raymond Michael Parrott
Navigator

20th September 1958

VX770 was the first Vulcan built and in 1952 made the types maiden flight in the hands of Avro Test Pilot, Wing Commander Roland "Roly" Falk. But it was as a development aircraft that VX770 would secure a much less desirable place in the history books.

In 1958, Rolls Royce at Hucknall was developing a more powerful engine to power the Vulcan known as the Conway. The Ministry of Supply, to assist the testing of the new engine, had lent them this aircraft. The testing was going well and the company had even managed to set a world record time flying to Rome.

On the day of the accident the civilian pilot, Keith Sturt, was on an engine test flight but he had also been given authority to perform a fly past at RAF Syerston's Battle of Britain Day Air Display. His display was supposed to consist of two fly pasts at 200-300 feet at a speed of no greater than 300 knots. In the event he flew by at around 420 knots at a height of just over 60 feet.

On completion of the fly past, the pilot pulled up steeply and entered a turn. At this point, the stresses on the airframe became too great and panels on the starboard wing began to delaminate. Once the internal structure of the wing became exposed to the airflow it began to disintegrate. The aircraft crashed at the end of Syerston's 07 runway, killing not only the entire crew, but also two airmen in the Runway Control Caravan and a third in a nearby rescue vehicle. A further airman who was also in the rescue vehicle was badly injured.

Raymond Parrott was the only member of RAF personnel on board the aircraft; he had been on temporary secondment to Rolls Royce from Scampton. It is not known where the other members of the crew are buried, but some of those killed on the ground are buried in Newark Cemetery.

There was a great deal of controversy surrounding this crash and many suggested that the aircraft was not strong enough to handle such powerful engines. Investigations established that the aircraft had been over-stressed to such a degree that it stood no chance of survival.

RAF Syerston had 20,000 visitors that day and the potential for a disaster of much greater proportions was evident to all.

On page 89 is a picture of the aircraft disintegrating and a plan of the crash site. Those who died alongside Flight Lieutenant Parrott were the pilot Mr Keith Sturt, the Second pilot Mr R W Ford and the Flight Engineer Mr W E Howkins. On the ground Sergeant E D Simpson, Sergeant C Hanson and SAC Tonks were killed. SAC Turnbull survived with injuries. An extract from the Board of Enquiry Report follows:

Mr. K. Sturt, a Rolls-Royce test pilot, was authorised to fly the Conway Vulcan VX 770 from Hucknall on Saturday 20th September 1958. The flight was primarily for the Conway engine test programme but at the conclusion of the flight, and if the timing was suitable, the aircraft was to carry out a fly past at Royal Air Force Syerston as part of Syerston's Battle of Britain At Home programme; after the fly past the aircraft was to return to Hucknall, an adjacent airfield.

Mr. Sturt was briefed for this fly past by Mr. Heyworth, Rolls-Royce Chief Test Pilot. It was to be two runs over Syerston at 200 to 300 feet and between 250 and 300 knots at 70% to 80% engine revolutions, making the same manoeuvre that Mr. Sturt had done at Farnborough Air Display on 7th September 1958.

At 1235Z Vulcan VX 770 called Syerston tower giving an ETA at Syerston of 1255Z. At 1250Z the Vulcan called Syerston Tower saying it was approaching from the West, height 250 feet for a fast run followed by a slow run. Syerston Tower acknowledged this message and told the Vulcan that the airfield was clear until 1300Z.

At 1257Z the Vulcan approached Syerston from the West and commenced a run up the main 25/07 runway at an approximate height of 80 feet (Appendix 5(iii)) and an estimated speed of 350 knots (1st witness).

A film taken at the time shows that when the aircraft was passing the Control Tower it started a roll to starboard and a slight climb; within 3/4 second a kink appeared in the starboard main plane leading edge approximately 9 feet outboard from the starboard engine intakes.

This was followed by a general stripping of the leading edge, the breaking off of the starboard wing tip and a general collapse of the main spar and wing structure between the spars. At this stage the wing was enveloped in a cloud of fuel vapour. The aircraft was now level, with the starboard wing broken off up to the undercarriage wheel well.

The Vulcan then went into a slight dive commencing a roll to port, which at 45 degree of bank, increased sharply at the same time shedding the tail fin. The remainder of the starboard wing was now on fire and the aircraft continued to roll to port with the nose lifting until the nose was vertical. The port wing leading edge began to crumble and fire broke out in the port wing.

The aircraft was now standing on its tail, travelling in plan form relative to the line of flight with the topside leading. The aircraft was then lost from view in an intense fire, reappearing with the nose pointing almost vertically downwards, having apparently continued its roll cum cartwheel. It continued in this attitude losing height until the topside of the nose struck the ground.

The port wing destroyed the fire/rescue Land Rover and runway controller's caravan, killing all three of the occupants and injuring a fourth. All four members of the Vulcan crew were killed. From the first indication of structural failure to the time of the crash was approximately 6 seconds. The wreckage trail extended over 1400 yards.

The aircraft disintegrating

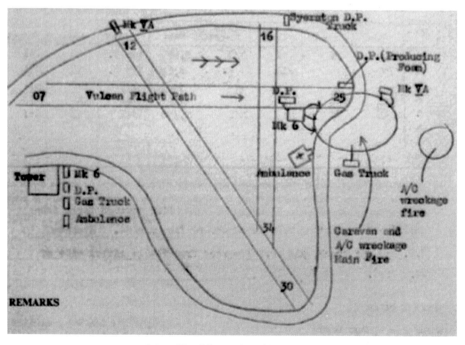

Original hand drawn plan of the crash site

Flight Lieutenant Victor Cyril Shuker

31st March 1960

Flight Lieutenant Shuker died in the RAF Hospital at Nocton Hall of natural causes. He had served at RAF Scampton as a Technical Armourer and was buried with appropriate military honours on the 4th April 1960.

Flight Sergeant Herbert McEntevy

30th November 1962

Flight Sergeant McEntevy, from Oldham, was a Fitter Armourer at Scampton and died of natural causes.

Leading Aircraftman Roy Ernest Thompson

30th December 1962

"Work hard, play hard" is the unwritten motto of the Royal Air Force and quite often the recreational side of service life can involve the consumption of a great deal of alcohol. Roy Thompson was a Sick Quarters Nursing Attendant who had no doubt decided to make the best of things despite being on duty over the festive period.

Having finished his duty shift, he went with his friend, Roger McNeal to the station's NAAFI bar. Here he consumed eight or nine pints of beer, before leaving for the night in good spirits.

Rather than going back to his room, he decided to sleep in Station Sick Quarters where he worked. On arriving, he found that the duty bunk was already occupied, so he decided to sleep in the heat treatment room.

The next morning, as a patient was being taken for heat treatment, it was discovered that Roy had died. A later post-mortem established that he had vomited in the night and because he was asleep, had inhaled the vomit and choked.

Like most people have done in the past, Roy had over done it on that night. However, unlike most people who wake up with nothing more than a monstrous hang-over, he had been very unlucky.

In tragic cases such as these, the margin between life and death can be very narrow indeed.

Corporal Thomas Joseph Caffery

14th December 1963

The cold war was at its height, only one year earlier the world had been on the brink of nuclear catastrophe as the Cuban missile crisis looked likely to lead to all-out war with the Soviets. Had war broken out, the Royal Air Force's nuclear strike bases would have been amongst the first targets.

Scampton was known to be high on the Soviet target list and to defend against air attack it was protected by Bloodhound surface to air missiles. These missiles flew at over two and a half times the speed of sound with a range of 85 Kilometres.

Corporal Caffery was serving with 141 Squadron which operated the Bloodhounds at Dunholme Lodge, he was killed in a road traffic accident on the Lincoln to Market Rasen Road.

Sergeant William Hart

28th December 1963

Sergeant Hart was a Royal Air Force Policeman and originally from Wigan. He died of natural causes.

Flight Sergeant Richard Humphrey Juliff

19th July 1965

Flight Sergeant Juliff was an aircraft fitter at RAF Scampton. He was a married man with one daughter; he died at the age of 46 from natural causes. Richard was a Welshman from Llanwono in Glamorgan.

Flight Lieutenant Norman Walter James Bevis

5th April 1966

Flight Lieutenant Bevis was a Vulcan pilot serving with 27 squadron at Scampton. After his death from natural causes, his wife Pauline presented an Altar Book inscribed with the RAF crest to the church. This book is still in use and can be seen by visitors.

The Altar Book in memory of Flight Lieutenant Bevis

Sergeant Jamie Albert Wardley BEM

25th June 1966

Sergeant Wardley, originally from Millwall collapsed in the early hours of the morning in the Sergeants' Mess. He was taken to the Station Sick Quarters but was pronounced dead on arrival.

Senior Aircraftman Rodney James Jarvis

5th September 1966

Rodney Jarvis, originally from Solihull near Birmingham, was the pillion passenger on a motorcycle. He and his friend Alan Martin, the driver of the bike, were leaving the car park of a hotel at Thorpe on the Hill, just to the south of Lincoln. As they pulled out on to the main road, they were in collision with a car. Coincidentally, another member of the RAF, Squadron Leader Thompson of RAF Uphavon drove the car. However, the two men did not know each other.

Rodney received relatively minor injuries in the crash and his broken thigh, whilst very painful, would not have caused anyone to fear for his life. Cruelly though, complications set in three days later and he died in Lincoln County Hospital as a result of globules of fat reaching his brain.

Chief Technician Patrick John Cairns

21st December 1966

Chief Technician Cairns was a Scotsman, known as Tam to his friends; he was married to his wife Sarah and had four children. Employed as an Aircraft Fitter at Scampton, he would no doubt have worked on the Vulcan that still formed a vital part of Britain's nuclear deterrent at the time. He died of natural causes aged 49.

Chief Technician David Horton Jarvis

27th December 1969

Chief Technician Jarvis died suddenly at the age of 48. He lived with his family in nearby Waddington village, suggesting a previous posting to the other major Vulcan base in the county. David was a Cornishman originally from Cambourne.

Flight Lieutenant Patrick Michael Nagaur

20th October 1973

Flight Lieutenant Nagaur was an Engineering Officer at Scampton and died of natural causes He was originally from Cedros in Trinidad.

Flight Lieutenant George Charles Barefoot

17th November 1973

Flight Lieutenant Barefoot died of natural causes whilst serving in the General Duties (Ground) branch at Scampton. George's hometown was Dover.

Sergeant Francis James Turner BEM

25th April 1974

As the recipient of a British Empire Medal, Sergeant Turner must have been a highly experienced and valued member of Scampton's aircraft engineering staff. Originally from Maidstone, he was an Aircraft Fitter and died of natural causes.

Senior Aircraftman Alastair Findlay

20th December 1976

The death of anyone at the age of 20 is difficult to accept, but when it is the result of someone else's reckless and criminal behaviour it must be particularly harrowing. Alastair Findlay was driving a small estate car with his two friends Kevan Robinson and Francis Reynolds. As he approached the roundabout between the Riseholme Road and Yarborough Crescent, Lincoln, they could have had no idea that a stolen vehicle was heading towards them being chased by the police.

Earlier in the evening, a soldier based at Kirton-in-Lindsey had stolen a 4-ton Bedford truck and headed towards Lincoln. The police had set-up a roadblock on the A15 at the Queen Elizabeth Junction, but the truck evaded this and continued its deadly journey towards the city. Just after midnight the truck hit Alastair's car with the police still in pursuit. Alastair received injuries which were to prove fatal; his two passengers were less seriously hurt. The 21-year-old soldier responsible for the crash was arrested and charged with driving offences.

Alastair and his passengers were all members of the famous 617 (Dambusters) Squadron. Members of the squadron as well as personnel from nearby RAF Waddington attended the funeral. Alastair had followed his father's footsteps into the RAF. He had been a Chief Technician and was living at nearby RAF Waddington.

Warrant Officer John Manchester

5th March 1977

On the 5th March 1940, 16 year-old John Manchester joined the Royal Air Force as a boy apprentice at RAF Halton. He served throughout World War II and was Mentioned in Dispatches during the North African campaign. At the cessation of hostilities he continued to serve in the Royal Air Force, marrying his wife Margaret in 1947 and having a son named John in 1948.

John and family moved to Scampton in November 1974. He was promoted to Warrant Officer on 1st January 1976 and worked as an Aircraft Fitter on 230 Operational Conversion Unit, servicing the Vulcan.

Whilst at Scampton, he was given the prestigious honour of being Chairman of the Sergeant's Mess Committee. Known as the grandfather of the mess, the Chairman of the Mess Committee was responsible for all aspects of life in the Sergeants' Mess and as such could wield considerable influence.

Just a few years from retirement, John and Margaret, who had spent all their married lives together in RAF Married Quarters, had bought a house in Welton, close to the base. However, after only three weeks in his new home, John died of a heart attack, 37 years to the day since he had originally joined the RAF.

Warrant Officer John Manchester

Flight Lieutenant Christopher Edwards
Flight Lieutenant Simon Farlow
Flight Lieutenant James Hamilton
Flight Lieutenant Nigel Thomas

11th August 1978

The Vulcan never failed to impress at air shows. The huge delta bomber, which combined fighter like performance with engines that could make spectators bones rattle, made a huge impression on all who saw it fly. I n d e e d , s uch was the popularity of this aircraft that even the Americans were clamouring to have it at their air shows. Naval Air Station Glenview, just outside Chicago, had become a regular on the Vulcan's show circuit where it was a star performer. When in America the Vulcan always impressed putting its equivalent, the American B52 Stratofortress, very much into second place.

On 11th August, despite the Vulcan getting old and entering its twilight years the upper echelons of the RAF command structure still wanted to maintain its prestige and it is possible that too much pressure was applied to perform. Vulcans were normally operated by constituted crews, that is to say that the same crew trained and flew together on every mission and this would normally also be true of the display crew. However in 1978 it was decided, quite late

XL390 on display at an air show in the UK prior to the accident

The crew (All four standing) immediately before the flight

in the day, to put together a crew specifically for the air show and it is fair to say, from relatives comments, that the crew themselves were not altogether comfortable with this. Having registered their objections, they did as ordered and began to prepare for the display in Chicago.

The day prior to the air show was Press Day and the crew of Vulcan XL390 prepared their aircraft for its display. As they taxied out for their flight all the crew must have felt the effect of the quite considerable pressure applied on them to perform. Not only were they expected to fly the display, they were expected to knock the socks off the finest the USAF had to offer. All this as a recently formed crew and in an aircraft that was reaching the end of its operational career.

The Vulcan began its "Dress rehearsal" display with a fast fly past followed by a wing-over, but for reasons which shall never be known it was unable to complete the manoeuvre with the height available and crashed killing all four crewmen. The residential area where the accident occurred was heavily populated, but the crash site was in the only clear area, a landfill site. Many of the locals felt that the crew must have used the last vestiges of control to direct the aircraft into the only clear area, sacrificing their own lives to save those on the ground.

The crew were buried at Scampton on the 18th August with the funerals being conducted by the Station's Chaplain, Squadron Leader the Reverend Nigel Bryan. The funeral was attended by most of 617 Squadron and the air show organiser Mr Don Jens, who was representing the Mayor of Chicago.

Sergeant Stuart Palmer

30th September 1978

Sergeant Palmer died of natural causes in Lincoln County Hospital. He was originally from Mansfield in Nottinghamshire.

Flight Lieutenant Russell Norman Todd
Mr Mark Andrew Todd

16th July 1979

The grave marker for Russell and Mark Todd

Of all the burials at Scampton, these two proved to be among the most difficult to research. The grave is not only unique in that it is a father and son who died on the same day, but also because it is the only RAF grave for a civilian in the churchyard.

Flight Lieutenant Todd was serving with 617 Squadron in the General Duties Branch and lived, together with his family, in Vulcan Close at RAF Scampton, which by coincidence is where a large part of this book was researched and written, as Gary Mennell lived for a period in the same street of RAF married quarters.

It was late on a Monday afternoon when Russell Todd (44) and his eighteen year old son Mark died in a car accident on the crossroads of the Welton to Spridlington Road and the Hackthorn to Cold Hanworth Road.

Although there were no witnesses to the crash, it would appear that Russell pulled out of a minor road into the path of a Land Rover being driven by 74 year-old Harold Fox. Mr Fox was a well known local businessman and although he survived the initial crash, he died of his injuries three days later.

Investigation of the crash site showed that recent road resurfacing had obliterated the give-way markings at the junction and overgrown hedges made visibility of the main road very difficult. At the inquest, verdicts of death by misadventure were recorded on the two drivers and a verdict of accidental death was recorded on Mark Todd.

Senior Aircraftman Kevin Michael Leng

25th November 1983

Even in peacetime, service in the Royal Air Force can be extremely stressful and for someone like Kevin Leng, who had an exemplary conduct record, he took it particularly hard when he found himself on the wrong side of service discipline.

At the time of his death, Kevin was the subject of a discipline enquiry at Scampton and although it was a relatively minor matter, which would not have had a long-term effect on his career, he seems to have worried about it much more than anybody realised.

Tragically, Kevin decided to hang himself from scaffolding outside his barrack block. Kevin had only been at Scampton for two months. A friend who had known him at that time had seen him the previous day and stated that Kevin had seemed quite happy, although he had been making a noose in the crew room for what he thought was a bit of fun.

In retrospect, this seems like an obvious plea for help, but the welfare system in the Royal Air Force was not as well established as it is in the modern Service. Today, stress is recognised as a real factor in Service life and one can only hope that the symptoms would be noticed and such a tragedy could be averted.

Flight Lieutenant Andrew James Potter
Corporal Kevin Turner

25th May 1986

The Vintage Pair had been thrilling air show crowds since 1972. The unique pairing of a Gloster Meteor and De Havilland Vampire were flown by the Royal Air Force's Central Flying School to remind the public of the pioneering days of jet aviation.

The Mildenhall Air Fete was always very well attended and the United States Air Force had earned a reputation for putting on one of the best shows in Britain. The Vintage Pair had become regular participants and were this day performing their usual display.

As the pair were flying in line astern, the Meteor leading the Vampire, they began a barrel roll. The Vampire could not match the Meteor's rate of roll and its tail fin struck the Meteor's left engine nacelle. After the collision, the Vampire pitched up and both crew ejected from their doomed aircraft. The Meteor rolled rapidly to the left and the pilot, Flight Lieutenant Potter, managed to temporarily roll the wings level.

The Vintage Pair

However, the damage to the aircraft was too severe for any pilot to cope with and eight seconds after the collision, the aircraft crashed. Because the Meteor was not equipped with ejector seats, both occupants had no chance of escape and were killed instantly.

At the time of the accident, it was customary for ground crew to be flown in each of the spare seats in the Vampire and Meteor. Sergeant Ball was in the Vampire and Kevin Turner in the Meteor on the fateful day.

Flight Lieutenant Potter was married with 2 children and lived just north of Scampton at Hemswell. He joined the Royal Air Force in June 1968 and was a Qualified Flying Instructor. Corporal Kevin Turner was originally from Kirk Hallam in Derbyshire. He had joined the Royal Air Force in 1978 as an aircraft Technician. His mother was quoted at the time as saying: "He joined the RAF when he was seventeen; it was what he had always wanted."

Flight Lieutenant Peter Wilson Stacey

30th May 1988

After the Vintage Pair disaster at Mildenhall, the Central Flying School had taken the decision to revive the historic flight with Meteor T7 WF791 taking the place of the lost aircraft. Almost exactly two years to the day since the previous accident, Flight Lieutenant Stacey was displaying the Meteor at Baginton near Coventry as part of the Warwickshire Air Pageant. Peter was three minutes

Meteor on display at Newark Air Museum

into his display when he entered a wing-over, the aim of which was to return to the crowd line and show the aircraft with its undercarriage and flaps down.

At first, all seemed normal, but as the undercarriage was lowered the nose of the aircraft pitched down and it dived into the ground. Once again, the Meteor's lack of ejector seats meant that the pilot was unable to escape and was killed on impact.

Those with experience of the Meteor when it was in frontline service with the Royal Air Force already knew what the board of enquiry would later discover. WF791 had fallen victim to the "Phantom Dive". At low speed, with air brakes out, the Meteor's elevators would become ineffective and the aircraft would pitch down. All too often this occurred at low level and many Meteor pilots of previous generations had been killed by the aircraft's worst vice

Video evidence later showed that the whole display had been flown with the air brakes out. For the majority of the display this did not prove to be a problem, but as the aircraft slowed in the wing-over and the undercarriage was lowered, all the criteria for a classic Phantom Dive were in place. It is likely that Flight Lieutenant Stacey never realised the air brakes were out as they were still in this state when found in the wreckage. What little control Peter had of the aircraft he used to steer it away from the Ernsford Grange housing estate on the edge of Coventry, crashing instead into a field. An eyewitness who saw the aircraft veer away from the houses was reported as saying: "If that is so, he was a very brave man indeed. If he had missed the trees he would certainly have hit the houses and the consequences would have been far worse." According to the local paper, reporting on the event, Peter had called the airport control tower and said "I'm coming down. I'm looking for open ground".

The memorial at the crash site   *The brass plaque in Scampton Church*

David Savery witnessed the tragic event as a child: He has written the following account on the Internet, but despite our best efforts we have been unable to trace him to discuss it. However we felt he would probably want his account to appear in this book. His appreciation of Peter Stacey's actions is clear to see:

101

I lived in the suburb of Ernesford Grange in Coventry as a kid, about three miles from Coventry Airport (better known then as Baginton Airport). In May 1988 my dad and I were watching the annual Warwickshire Air Pageant from our back garden. It was hot and sunny and our proximity to the airfield meant we had a good free view of all manner of wonderful aircraft flying over our house as they took off from Baginton and turned around to be back on the return flight path.

Me and my dad stood in the sunshine of the back garden and watched that Meteor streak across the blue sky from left to right with the sunshine bouncing off its frame. Then it turned towards us and lowered altitude. It didn't register with me at the time and in fact, it wasn't until I heard my dad telling the crash investigators later, that when it was just a couple of hundred metres above ground level and just a couple of hundred metres away, it was silent.

The roar of it's engines had stopped and it was losing altitude and heading directly for our housing estate. Some people say the Meteor had fallen below stall speed by then, but I know what I saw.

Flt Lt Stacey knew if he hit the houses there would be massive loss of life and he took the split second decision to nose dive the stricken Meteor into a patch of open ground between the Willenhall and Ernesford Grange housing estates. I saw the Meteor in a controlled descent until that sudden nose dive.

Sadly, the fuel laden plane exploded on impact into a massive fireball which bathed us in heat and left us knowing there was no hope of Flt. Lt. Stacey surviving. My father and I both ran out of the front of the house and around to the end of the road. The air was thick with smoke and the smell of aircraft fuel.

A police car which happened to have been travelling down Lang Bank Avenue was already parked up with two stunned looking Police officers radioing for help and telling the residents to keep back.

A WM Travel bus had swerved to a stop on Langbank Avenue ahead of the Police car and according to the Coventry Evening Telegraph the driver had feared the plane was going to hit his double decker.

There's no doubt in my mind that Flt Lt Stacey in his final seconds, saw that bus, the police car and the people in their gardens enjoying the bank holiday sunshine. Maybe he even saw me. Whatever he saw in those final moments, he bravely sacrificed his own life to avoid a major disaster.

Over twenty years on, there are those of us who still remember.

Certainly the local people were satisfied that Peter was a hero and had saved countless lives. His funeral was attended by representatives of Coventry Council, West Midlands Police and Baginton Airport Fire Brigade. Councillor Bill McKernan said "Flight Lieutenant Stacey died hopefully in the knowledge that he had saved the lives of many people. Undoubtedly he was an extremely brave man, because he kept his cool and took the plane away from homes".

A Memorial to his actions was placed at the site of the crash and in Scampton Church by the grateful residents.

Flight Lieutenant Stacey had served in the Royal Air Force for 10 years; he was employed at Scampton as a Qualified Flying Instructor and was single. His funeral was attended by his elderly mother Ella Stacey who arrived on the arm of her remaining son Clive who lived in South Africa. The RAF Scampton Chaplain, Reverend John Betteley led the service and in his address said " Peter was a man whose joy of flying was paramount to his life. I doubt whether he would have wanted to end his life in any other way than at the controls of an aircraft"

Flight Lieutenant David Laird Ferguson Adam

18th March 1991

Canberra WJ877

The Canberra was another aircraft that belonged to the pioneering era of jet aviation. The Canberra had its origins as an aircraft designed in World War II, but first flew in 1949. By the time of the accident, the type had seen over 40 years of RAF service. This however, did not come without it too exposing its vices. The aircraft was particularly difficult to handle at low speed on one engine. If a Canberra lost an engine at low-level and the pilot did not apply rudder correctly to counter the effect, the aircraft would roll rapidly and in many cases crash.

On the afternoon of 18th March 1991, Flight Lieutenant Adam was the Navigator of Canberra T4 (WJ877). He and his pilot Flight Lieutenant Stephen Wilkinson, a

Qualified Flying Instructor (QFI) were tasked with flying RAF Wyton's Station Commander, Group Captain Reginald McKendrick, to a meeting at RAF Kinloss in northern Scotland. He was second pilot and to make the most of the flight, it was decided that a check would be conducted on him to see how he would handle an engine failure after take-off. Such checks are a routine part of any pilot's life.

The aircraft was seen to take-off normally and the wheels were retracted. As the aircraft passed the air traffic control tower, it rolled to the left. This was stopped but it then rolled rapidly to the right and crashed from a height of 150 feet.

Although two of the crew did attempt to eject, there wasn't sufficient time for their ejector seats to work and all three crew members were killed. As well as Flight Lieutenant Adam, Group Captain McKendrick and Flight Lieutenant Stephen Wilkinson also lost their lives.

Further tragedy was narrowly avoided as the aircraft crashed across the busy Huntingdon to March road at rush hour. Cambridgeshire Police said of the accident: "Normally the road would have been full of cars going home at the time of the crash, but there was a gap in the traffic and the road was unusually empty."

The subsequent investigation was hampered by the lack of a flight data recorder, but it was thought that the Station Commander anticipated the simulated engine failure and applied rudder slightly too early. As the aircraft rolled to the left he realised his mistake and eased off on the rudder. However, by this time the asymmetric power of the one remaining engine was beginning to take effect. When he re-applied the left rudder to counter the roll to the right, it was too late and the crash was inevitable.

A typical Canberra crew at Scampton with their aircraft

Flight Lieutenant David Laird Ferguson Adam

Bibliography

We are indebted to the authors of the following books which assisted and / or enabled us in our research:

Airfield Focus, Scampton Revisited	Stewart A Scott
Air Force Memorials of Lincolnshire	M Ingham
Beware of the Dog at War	J Ward
Bomber Command War Diaries	M Middlebrook and C Everitt
Bomber Command War Losses (all)	W R Chorley
Bomber County	T N Hancock
Fighter Command Losses (all)	Norman L R Franks
Final Landings	Colin Cummings
Hampden Crash Log	Nicholas Roberts
Hell on High Ground	D W Earl
Last Take-off	Colin Cummings
Lincolnshire Air War Books 1&2	S Finn
Luftwaffe Losses over Northumberland and Durham	Bill Norman
RAF Coastal Command Losses	Ross McNeill
The Gisela Tragedy	I Haythorne
The Hampden File	H Moyle
The Price of Peace	Colin Cummings
They Shall Not Grow Old	L Allison and H Hayward
To Fly no more	Colin Cummings
83 Squadron 1917-1969	R G Low and F E Harper

We are further grateful to the following sources of information:

The families, friends and acquaintances of those in the cemetery
All those who have contributed accounts and memories
RAF Scampton Historical Museum and Mr Mervyn Hallam
The National Archive, Kew
The 49 Squadron Association
The Lincolnshire Echo
Lincoln Libraries and their staff
The Station Commander, RAF Scampton
Also many thanks go to Marjorie Keast for Proof Reading.

The RAF Scampton Historical Museum

To celebrate the history of Scampton a station museum was created in August 1993. It is currently housed in one of the original World War Two hangars and contains over 400 artefacts (including a Blue Steel Missile) which will be of interest to aviation enthusiasts around the world. The Museum is run on a voluntary basis and no admission is charged. All they ask is that you contact the curator prior to your visit as the museum is not permanently manned and due to current security measures, access to the station is not possible without prior arrangement.

Curator: Mr Mervyn Hallam. Tel 01522 683856/731462
or Roger Crisp Tel 01522 500738
e.mail: mervhallam@hotmail.com

The Museum has been vital to our research and we are only too pleased to commend it and suggest you arrange a visit - perhaps to coincide with your visit to Scampton Churchyard.

This view is of a model Lancaster made by an enthusiast and kindly donated to the museum. It's a finely detailed scale model of S for Sugar that completed 137 sorties and now resides in the RAF Museum at Hendon.

One of the many rooms of exhibits in the Museum